Conversational Style: Analyzing Talk Among Friends

Language and Learning for Human Service Professions

A Series of Monographs
edited by

Cynthia Wallat, Florida State University
and
Judith Green, The Ohio State University

Volumes in the series include:

Marilyn Cochran-Smith • *The Making of a Reader* (1984)

Deborah Tannen • *Conversational Style: Analyzing Talk Among Friends* (1984)

Celia Genishi and Anne Haas Dyson • *Language Assessment in the Early Years* (1984)

Elliot G. Mishler • *The Discourse of Medicine: Dialectics of Medical Interviews* (1984)

William Corsaro • *Friendship and Peer Culture in the Early Years* (1984)

Conversational Style: Analyzing Talk Among Friends

DEBORAH TANNEN

Georgetown University

Ablex Publishing Corporation
Norwood, New Jersey 07648

Fourth printing 1990

Printed in the United States of America

Library of Congress Cataloging in Publication Data

Tannen, Deborah.
  Conversational style.

  Includes bibliographical references and index.
  1. Conversation.   2. Discourse analysis.   I. Title.
P95.45.T36   1983   001.54′2′019   83-25697
ISBN 0-89391-188-7
ISBN 0-89391-200-X pbk.

Ablex Publishing Corporation
355 Chestnut Street
Norwood, New Jersey 07648

To Karl

A pause in the wrong place, an intonation misunderstood, and a whole conversation went awry.

—E. M. Forster, *A Passage to India*

Contents

CHAPTER 3
The Participants in Thanksgiving Dinner   44

CHAPTER 4
Linguistic Devices in Conversational Style   54

CHAPTER 5
Narrative Strategies   97

CHAPTER 6
Irony and Joking   130

CHAPTER 7
Summary of Style Features   144

CHAPTER 8
The Study of Coherence in Discourse   152

Preface to the Series
Language and Learning for Human Service Professions

This series of monographs is intended to make the theories, methods, and findings of current research on language available to professional communities that provide human services. From a theoretical and practical point of view, focus on language as a social process means exploring how language is actually used in everyday life.

Communication between and among adults and children, professionals and clients, and teachers and students, as well as the effect of changing technology on communication in all these contexts, has become the object of study in disciplines as varied as anthropology, cognitive psychology, cognitive science, education, linguistics, social psychology, and sociology. The series provides a forum for this research which analyzes talk in homes, communities, schools, and other institutional settings. The aim is to shed light on the crucial role of language and communication in human behavior.

The monographs in the series will focus on three main areas:

- Language and Social Relationships
- Language and Helping Professions
- Language and Classroom Settings

We hope that these books will provide rich and useful images of and information about how language is used.

Judith Green and Cynthia Wallat

Acknowledgments

No standard acknowledgment, no usual thanks, can express my gratitude to the three whose work in linguistics furnished the foundations of my own, as they furnished models as scholars, teachers, critics, and friends: Wallace Chafe, John Gumperz, and Robin Tolmach Lakoff.

My debt to Robin Lakoff goes yet further back; her course at the 1973 Linguistic Institute in Ann Arbor planted the seeds of most of the ideas developed here and prompted me to pursue the study of linguistics. That same summer I had the rare good fortune to take Introduction to Linguistics with A. L. Becker, whose humanistic approach to language and linguistics has continued to inspire and inform my work, and to hear Emanuel Schegloff's public lecture, my first intoxicating and, as it turned out, addictive taste of conversational microanalysis, suggesting the arcane in the commonplace and order where there had seemed chaos (the stuff of which both science and wonder are made).

I give thanks, too, to the Thanksgiving celebrants, my friends who unwittingly (albeit willingly) became my data. Not only their initial and continuing consent but their uniform patience and insight during playback, made this study possible.

My sincere thanks go, also, to the organizations and the people associated with them who offered invaluable support: the Danforth Foundation and the Institute of Human Learning at the University of California, Berkeley, for the initial writing, and Georgetown University for a summer research grant that helped free me for revision.

I am grateful to Karl Goldstein, Karen Beaman, and Heidi Hamilton for help in double checking the transcription, and to many who made invaluable critical comments on earlier versions, including A. L. Becker, Erving Goffman, Dell Hymes, Dennis Jarrett, June McKay, Marilyn Merritt, Stephen Murray, Emanuel Schegloff, Ron Scollon, and Cynthia Wallat, and also to many who made equally invaluable uncritical comments, which encouraged me to publish this.

I want to thank Tom Brazaitis for helping me master my Apple and Epson. And finally, for support of every kind, I want to thank those who started it all and continue to be my most dependable and beloved models of two conversational styles, my parents Dorothy and Eli Tannen.

Preface to the Volume

This book presents a linguistic approach to analyzing conversation. It includes two alternate introductions: one for nonlinguists explaining the concept and workings of conversational style in lay terms, and one for linguists which includes relevant literature review, explains my definition of and approach to the analysis of conversational style, introduces the stylistic features examined in the study, and discusses some theoretical, methodological and ethical issues raised by the study.

The body of the analysis is presented in Chapters 3 through 7. The last chapter, The Study of Coherence in Discourse, discusses the relationship between ordinary conversation and literary language and suggests a theoretical approach to the study of coherence in discourse. Appendices list further readings in the fields to which this study is relevant: sociolinguistics, discourse analysis, and cross-cultural communication.

This study identifies and illustrates the linguistic features that make up the conversational styles of six speakers, as recorded in two and a half hours of talk at a Thanksgiving dinner. It demonstrates the (positive) effects of the use of these features in interaction among those whose styles are relatively similar, as compared to the (negative) effects of their use among those whose styles differ, with respect to the features studied.

I envision this book serving what may sound at first like a preposterously broad audience:

1. Lay interested readers—anyone with a curiosity about language and communication.
2. Professionals in any field in which dealing with other people is a requirement, for example, therapists, doctors, lawyers, teachers, salespeople.
3. Students in introductory courses in sociolinguistics, discourse analysis, and cross-cultural communication.
4. Students in graduate courses in conversational analysis.
5. Scholarly audiences in discourse theory.

I believe this book can reach such a diverse audience because I have written it as plainly as I could, using nontechnical terms wherever possible, and explaining technical terms when they appear. Furthermore, I have added sections that may be read by some readers and skipped by others.

Thus, readers in the first and second categories (lay and nonlinguist professional audiences) may want to read Chapter 1, Introduction for Nonlinguists, and the analysis chapters (3 through 7). Readers in the third category (students in introductory courses) may wish to read either or both of the introductions (in this they will be guided by their instructors) plus the analysis chapters. They may refer as well to the list of supplementary readings in the Appendices which, together with the analysis chapters and the Appendix outlining steps to be followed in analyzing a conversation, furnish a complete introductory course to the fields named. Finally, scholars in categories 4 and 5 may read the Introduction for Linguists as well as the analysis chapters and the final chapter, The Study of Coherence in Discourse.

KEY TO TRANSCRIPTION CONVENTIONS

.. noticeable pause or break in rhythm (less than 0.5 second)

... half second pause, as measured by stop watch

an extra dot is added for each half second of pause, hence,

.... full second pause

..... second and a half pause, and so on

´ marks primary stress

` marks secondary stress

<u>underline</u> marks emphatic stress

CAPS mark very emphatic stress

' marks high pitch on word

⌐marks high pitch on phrase, continuing until punctuation

ˌ marks low pitch on word

ʟmarks low pitch on phrase, continuing until punctuation

. marks sentence-final falling intonation

? marks yes/no question rising intonation

- marks a glottal stop, or abrupt cutting off of sound, as in "uh-oh"

: indicates lengthened vowel sound (extra colons indicate greater lengthening)

→ at left of line highlights point of analysis

→ at right of line indicates sentence continues without break in rhythm (look for next line)

, marks phrase-final intonation (more to come)

musical notation is used for amplitude and appears under the line:

   p piano (spoken softly)

   pp pianissimo (spoken very softly)

   f forte (spoken loudly)

   ff fortissimo (spoken very loudly)

   acc spoken quickly

   dec spoken slowly

   The above notations continue until punctuation, unless otherwise noted

/?/ indicates transcription impossible

/words/ within slashes indicate uncertain transcription

[brackets] are used for comments on quality of speech and context

⌐Brackets between lines indicate overlapping speech
ʟTwo people talking at the same time

Brackets on two lines⌐
                     ʟindicate second utterance

latched onto first, without perceptible pause

CHAPTER 1

Introduction for Nonlinguists

This is a book that was conceived and written as a scholarly study in linguistics. However, it can be read—indeed, it has happily been read—by nonlinguists and nonacademics who have an interest in the field of linguistics (or its subfield, sociolinguistics) and those who have an interest only in the practical business of communication.

The book is about conversational style. This refers to aspects of talk that have been observed by scholars but are also apparent to many nonscholars who are people watchers by nature. First, as sociologist Erving Goffman continually illustrated in his work, when people talk they communicate not only information but images of themselves. Second, as demonstrated by the work of anthropological linguist John Gumperz and others, many of the basic elements of how people talk, which seem self-evidently appropriate, in fact differ from one person to the next and from one group to the next. Ways of showing that you're interested, glad, or angry; how and when to tell a joke or a story; when to start talking and when to stop; when (or whether) it's okay to talk at the same time as someone else or to interrupt; how loud to talk; what intonation to use—these and many other features of language are not normally questioned by speakers, but they can be very different, depending on a speaker's individual habits as well as such differences as gender, ethnicity, class, and regional background.

Conversational style is not something extra or fancy, as if some people speak with style and others speak plainly. Rather it is made up of the basic tools with which people communicate. Anything that is said must be said in some way, and that way is style. In order to understand any words spoken, you need to know how the words are meant; is the speaker joking, scolding, being friendly or rude? You need to know what the other person is trying to do by what she or he says. The way that these intentions are communicated are the features of conversational style: tone of voice, pausing, speeding up and slowing down, getting louder and softer, and so on—all the elements that make up not only what you say but how you say it.

As linguist Robin Lakoff has repeatedly shown, people more often than not do not say what they mean—at least not in so many words—because there are important social reasons for not doing so. In talking to each other, people are caught (as Ron Scollon has pointed out) in a double bind, a situation, according to the concept developed by the anthropologist Gregory Bateson, in which a person must obey two conflicting commands and cannot just leave the situation. Obeying one means disobeying the other. In communication, these two commands are the need to be connected to other people, and the need to be independent. The need to be connected to other people comes from the danger of isolation. On a very real level, a human being alone would die. But there is also a danger in connection. If human beings get too close, the needs and wants of others can be imposing, or even engulfing, and again the individual dies, at least as an individual. We do not want to feel alone in the world, but we do not want to be engulfed by others either. Human relationships become a matter of juggling the need for involvement with other people and the need to be independent; in other words, we juggle the need for and danger of being close. This book analyzes and illustrates the different ways that different speakers honor these needs in conversation, through their conversational styles.

My analysis of conversational style is based on the talk that took place during two hours and forty minutes of conversation at a Thanksgiving dinner in Berkeley, California in 1978. There were six participants, three of whom (including me) were born and raised in New York City, two in southern California, and one in London, England. Analysis of the taped and transcribed conversation shows that in some ways, the three speakers from New York share conversational style. They use features and devices in similar ways that have a positive effect with each other and a negative effect with the others. But this is not to imply that their styles really were the same. Each person's style is unique; each one used devices in differing combinations and in different ways.

I had initially intended this to be a study of the styles of all participants, but the conversation itself made this impossible. It turned out (and this came as a surprise to me when I asked them several months later what they recalled about this Thanksgiving) that the non-New York participants had perceived the conversation as 'New York', and they had felt out of their element. Because the New Yorkers present tended to expect shorter pauses between speakers' turns at talk, the non-New Yorkers had a harder time saying something before a faster talker had begun to talk. (The problem was not insurmountable, because everyone present talked at one time or another.) Furthermore, because the New Yorkers had different ideas about how talk proceeded from topic to topic, the non-New Yorkers were often puzzled about what would be an appropriate comment, or what was appropriate about the comments of others. So, inevitably, this book ended up as a study of one style, what I call a high-involvement style, which tended to characterize the speakers from New York. (Bear in mind that each speaker's style is unique, that there are many New Yorkers whose styles are very different from those of the speakers in this study, and that there are many people, not from New York, whose styles are similar to that of these New Yorkers.)

The point is not that a New York style is inherently dominating. This is a stereotype that many people hold, which I hope partially to explain but not to buttress. Rather, as the linguist Edward Sapir (1958:542) observed, 'It is always the variation that matters, never the objective behavior'. In other words, the New Yorkers were faster relative to the others present in this conversation. But in another setting or in conversation with other people, their styles might look very different. The same speakers who had a hard time getting a word in edgewise in this conversation might come out looking like conversational bullies in talk with others who tend to be a bit slower-paced than they, and the ones who 'dominated' here might be effectively locked out in conversation with others who expect slightly shorter pauses between turns than they.

To illustrate, a running joke between my colleague Ron Scollon and me is that I tend to cut him off in just the way I have described myself and other New Yorkers doing at Thanksgiving. When we talk to each other, I am a fast talker and he is a slow one. But in a videotape he made about communication in Alaska, where he works, he mentions that when he talks to native Alaskan Indians, they never get a chance to talk because they expect longer pauses between speaking turns than he does. In Alaska he is a fast talker. On the other hand, in some situations I have a hard time getting a turn to talk. For example, in public settings, I feel it impolite to raise my hand while someone else is talking, with the frequent result that those who do not wait to raise their hands get to talk before anyone knows that I have something to say. This phenomenon is important to remember because we are all inclined to think of our own behavior as being reactions to other people's behavior ('I can't get a word in edgewise with him'), but we tend to think of other people's behavior as absolute ('He's a big talker,' or 'He's the silent type'.)

In other words, it is important to remember that the workings of conversational style illustrated in this book are relative processes, not objective behaviors. In a different setting with different others, each of these people's styles would look very different.

Why is it necessary to be aware of conversational style? Who cares? When everyone's style is the same (which probably never happens but might be more closely approached in a homogeneous society) there may be no need to know about it. Use of stylistic features that are automatic, in speaking and in interpreting others' speech, would not lead anyone far astray. But in a heterogeneous society, any one in which people come into contact with others from more or less different backgrounds, automatic use of conversational style leads everyone very far astray. Everyone is judging others and being judged by their ways of talking. If those ways reflect different habits and expectations, then people are continually misjudged and misunderstood. You try to be nice and are judged pushy; you try to be considerate and are judged cold. You try to make a good impression in a job interview or at a cocktail party and see that the other person is annoyed rather than charmed.

The consequences of such misunderstandings vary, depending on the seriousness of the encounter. If the setting is a cocktail party, you may simply move on and find someone else whose style is closer to yours (and possibly risk the accusation of being clannish or cliquish). If the setting is a job interview or other key situation such as those anthropologist Frederick Erickson has called 'gatekeeping', the consequences may be dire. If the setting is your work place, you risk misjudging the people you work with, and being misjudged. If you have moved to a different part of the country or a different country altogether, the repeated misunderstandings may make you draw negative conclusions about your new home. If the setting is your very own home, and the person with whom these misunderstandings arise is your living and loving partner, you may feel that you are losing your mind (or your partner has already lost his or hers, or has bad intentions). An awareness of conversational style may not prevent misunderstandings from arising, but it can help people understand them after the fact without having to see themselves or others as crazy or mean.

I hope that an understanding of patterns of everyday talk will free the common speaker, as well, of the burden imposed by nonlinguist language pundits (both professional and familial) who continually excoriate them for speaking the way people talk instead of the way people write. Most of us, poor creatures, are easy victims of linguistic insecurity. I see this continually when I am told by new acquaintances who have just learned that I am a linguist that, alas, they do not know how to speak English—the very English that they are perfectly well using to make this confession, which they have learned in the course of interaction, just as they learned to walk and to cook and to build things. How easily people accuse themselves (and their spouses and friends and enemies) of making mistakes, even if those mistakes are made regularly by most of the people they talk to. I hope this book will be a first step toward understanding that the language as written in essays is one system, and the language as spoken in casual conversation is another, and that the language of conversation should be understood rather than bludgeoned with the club of the language of essays. Of course there are times when people make mistakes (grammatical as well as social), or genuinely intend to be rude or ornery, or just are not very nice people. But just as often, in fact more often, people talk the way they do for very good social reasons, and others think them wrong, ornery, odd, or particularly charming when they are simply conducting conversational business as usual, instinctively using the features of conversational style as they seem self-evidently appropriate.

Conversational style and how it works will be presented in the Thanksgiving conversation. At this point, if you can't wait for dinner, you may turn to Chapter 3 to meet the participants. (You may need to be reminded of who is who later, so Appendix II lists them for easy reference.) If, however, before or after reading the analysis of talk that went on at this dinner, you would like to read more of the theoretical background and implications of conversational style linguistics, you may read parts or all of Chapter 2, Introduction for Linguists.

CHAPTER 2

Introduction for Linguists

More and more attention within linguistics is turning toward discourse analysis, which in many cases means and in most cases includes conversational analysis.[1] Fillmore (1974) is representative in asserting, 'The language of face-to-face conversation is the basic and primary use of language, all others being best described in terms of their manner of deviation from that base'.

Conversation, however, is an awesome area of investigation because it is so vast and elusive. It is tempting merely to record a segment of conversation, transcribe it, and then gloss it (supply a running commentary or concordance) and leave it at that. This is too often done and is what gives discourse analysis a bad name. On the other hand, it is easy to dismiss conversational analysis as 'ad hoc' and 'interpretive' (this last wielded as a damning epithet). To dismiss the possibility of studying conversation because it is too diffuse and not readily quantifiable would be to dismiss the basic material of interaction, indeed of humanness. It would be irresponsible. To prohibit the use of our most basic tool, our personal experience as veterans of human interaction, as

---

[1]The term *discourse* has been variously used to mean conversation; written texts; two hypothetical sentences in sequence; or (as I use it) all of the above, that is, anything beyond the sentence.

experienced practitioners of conversation, would be reckless. The solution lies in some combination of interpretation (which has a long scholarly tradition under the more impressive-sounding name *hermeneutics*) and quantification, plus a method for developing and correcting interpretations.

This book presents such a possible mode of analysis, a method developed under the influence of John Gumperz with theoretical underpinnings influenced by Gumperz as well as Robin Lakoff, whose work on communicative style has been the most direct influence on my concept of conversational style.

Conversational Style as Semantics

This book, then, is a presentation of a model of conversational analysis. It is a step toward the goal of understanding conversational interaction: what accounts for the impressions made when speakers use specific linguistic devices? What accounts for the mutual understanding or lack of it in conversation?

It is impossible to posit a one-to-one relationship between linguistic form and meaning (or, put another way, language form and function). The same linguistic and, inseparably, paralinguistic form can have different meanings depending on the speaker (who is saying it) and the context (how the speaker perceives the situation and the relationships among participants).

Hymes (1973) reminds us that the field of semantics itself began as a separate area of study, because neither linguistics nor ethnography was prepared to deal with it, but eventually it was taken into the domain of linguistics proper. Similarly, he suggests, the field of sociolinguistics should, in time, 'lose itself and its name in the standard practice of linguistics and ethnography' (p. 313), for 'the issue again is the study of meaning, only now, social meaning' (p. 325). In fact, there can hardly be any meaning other than social meaning. As a generation of generative semanticists discovered (with the result that they metamorphosed into pragmaticists), hardly a sentence can be seen as having a crystalline meaning that cannot be changed by the positing of a different context for it.

In other words, an alternative title for this book could have been *The Semantics of Conversational Style,* for the basic question at issue is really semantics: How do people communicate and interpret meaning in conversation?

Style

Much has been written about *style,* a term that Hymes (1974a) aptly calls protean. (Discussions of the term can be found in Ervin-Tripp 1972; Hymes 1974a,b; Romaine and Traugott 1981.) Ervin-Tripp (1972:235) defines style as 'the co-occurrent changes at various levels of linguistic structure within one language' and suggests that linguistic choices are made on two levels. Syntagmatic relations, following rules of co-occurrence, result in identifiable styles. Paradigmatic relations, following rules of alternation, result in choices among styles and make possible style-switching, on the model of code-switching. Ervin-Tripp's notion of style as generated by co-occurrence constraints corresponds to what Hymes identifies as 'registers', accounting for what is often thought of as formal vs. informal speech. My use of *style* includes this and refers more generally to the choices Ervin-Tripp identifies as alternation, resulting in the mix of devices speakers use in different contexts.

Hymes notes that a speech community is comprised of a set of styles, with *style* used simply in 'the root sense of a way or mode of doing something' (p. 434). Thus, speech styles are simply 'ways of speaking.' Like Hymes, I use *style* to refer to no more nor less than a way of doing something. It is crucial to make clear that *style* does not refer to a special way of speaking, as if one could choose between speaking plainly or speaking with style. Plain is as much a style as fancy. Anything that is said or done must be said or done in some way, and that way constitutes style. If you sit in a chair, motionless, you are sitting in a certain position, dressed in certain clothes, with a certain expression on your face. Thus you sit in the chair in your own style. You can no more talk without style than you can walk or sit or dress without style. Anything you say must be said at a certain rate, at a certain pitch and amplitude, in certain intonation, at a certain point in interaction. All these and countless other choices determine the effect of an utterance in interaction and influence judgments that are made both about what is said and about the speaker who says it. All these and countless other necessary choices determine a speaker's style.

In other words, style is not something extra added on like frosting on a cake. It is the stuff of which the linguistic cake is made.

In an article originally written in 1927, Sapir (1958:542) included style as the fifth level of speech contributing to judgments of personality. Devoting only a paragraph to it, he defined style as 'an everyday facet of speech that characterizes both the social group and the individual'. Here are raised two basic issues related to style. The first is the fact that conversational style, a person's way of talking, results in judgments about his or her personality. I often catch myself saying in explanation of myself or others, 'Oh, that's just his/her/my style'. Yet the issue is far more complicated than that. In a way, if that is a person's style, then that is also the person's personality. This is an issue that will not be resolved here but will repeatedly be suggested by the analysis and discussion of the styles of the participants in Thanksgiving dinner.

Speech—the use of language in all its phonological, lexical, syntactic, prosodic, and rhythmic variety—is one element of a range of behavioral characteristics that make up personal style. It would be ideal, ultimately, to link an analysis of language use with a comprehensive analysis of other elements of behavior. At the very least, a linguistic analysis should correlate verbal with proxemic, kinesic, and other nonverbal communicative channels such as facial expression and gesture. For example, as will be illustrated presently, Lakoff (1978) relates linguistic to personality style in the psychoanalytic paradigm. In this book, however, I concentrate on the linguistic channel per se, because this is a natural starting place for a linguist, and also because the Thanksgiving conversation was audiotaped but not videotaped.

Individual and Social Differences

The second issue raised by Sapir's observation is that of individual vs. social differences. As Sapir points out, it is necessary to know what is 'unmarked', that is, what is conventionalized within a community, in order to know what special meaning an individual may be intentionally or unintentionally communicating by diverging from convention. Everyone, I believe, has had the experience of knowing someone and later meeting someone else—a family member or another person from the same part of the country or the same foreign country—and being overwhelmed by how similar the new person is to the known one. In other words, features that one had considered unique to the individual suddenly are seen as shared, or social, phenomena.

Gumperz and Tannen (1979) show that impressions of style grow out of the use of linguistic devices to signal how an utterance is meant. They attempt to identify the level of signaling on which individual as compared to social differences arise. For example, speakers from different countries (e.g. from the work of Gumperz, speakers of Indian as opposed to British English) may differ with respect to basic conversational control devices, for example, whether they use increased amplitude to get the floor or use it as an expressive show of anger. In contrast, speakers from different regions of the same country (e.g. from the work of Tannen, speakers from New York as opposed to Boston, or men as opposed to women) may differ about when and how to apply similar devices, for example irony or indirectness.

Of course the issue is not so simply settled. Each person's individual style is a combination of features learned in interaction with others (hence, social) plus features developed idiosyncratically. Perhaps the impression of individual style results from the unique combination and deployment of socially learned features.

The Acquisition of Style

Before proceeding to the background of relevant research and then to the analysis of conversational data, it may be useful to say something about how style is learned. Style is not a sophisticated skill learned late or superimposed on previously acquired linguistic forms. Rather, it is learned as an integral part of linguistic knowledge.

Recent research on developmental pragmatics (for example, papers collected in Ervin-Tripp and Mitchell-Kernan 1977 and Ochs and Schieffelin 1979; Ochs 1982) documents how children learn to use devices that constitute style. Anderson (1977) shows that children by the age of four appropriately use stylistic variables (syntax, lexical choice, politeness forms, intonation, and so on) in role playing puppet characters of different social status. Schieffelin (1979) demonstrates, based on her research among the Kaluli of Papua New Guinea, that children learn social knowledge simultaneously with language structure. As she puts it, they simultaneously learn what to say, how to say it, and how to feel about it, which is entailed inevitably in the way to say it.

Schieffelin's findings for first language learning correspond to those of Wong Fillmore (1976, 1979) for second language learning, which show that newly arrived Spanish-speaking children in a California bilingual classroom learned English by learning formulaic phrases, complete with intonation patterns and gestures and associated with use in specific social contexts. In other words, style is learned as part of the intrinsically social process of language learning. (For a cogent presentation of this view see Cook-Gumperz 1975.)

Stylistic Strategies: Involvement and Considerateness

I shall suggest in the forthcoming analysis that individual stylistic choices are not random but constrained by overriding stylistic strategies that are conventionalized ways of serving identifiable universal human needs. The work of R. Lakoff on communicative style, with its beginnings in her work on 'the logic of politeness' (1973), introduces the notion of stylistic strategies.

Lakoff observes that speakers regularly and intentionally refrain from saying what they mean in service of the higher goal of politeness in its broadest sense, that is, to fulfill the social function of language. She devised a system that represents the universal logic underlying specific linguistic choices (i.e. indirectness, preference for particular lexical or syntactic forms) in the form of three principles originally called Rules of Politeness (later called Rules of Rapport).

1. Don't impose (Distance)
2. Give options (Deference)
3. Be friendly (Camaraderie)

In choosing the form of an utterance, speakers observe one or another of these rules. Furthermore, each of these rules, when applied in interaction, creates a particular stylistic effect, as indicated by the terms in parentheses. That is, preference for honoring one or another of these politeness principles results in a communicative strategy that makes up style. Conversely, conversational style results from habitual use of linguistic devices motivated by these overall strategies. Distance, deference, and camaraderie, then, refer to styles associated with particular notions of politeness. (Note that these terms are part of Lakoff's system and do not necessarily have the connotations associated with their use in popular parlance.)

In this system, then, distance (resulting from application of R1, 'Don't impose') typically applies in a formal situation. It governs the use of technical language. In addition, it is the principle by which one would choose an indirect expression of preferences, so as not to impose one's will on others. When I ask my guest, 'Would you like something to drink,' the person who replies, 'Thank you, that would be nice', may be seen to employ such a strategy. The reply is depersonalized in a sense. It should be emphasized, incidentally, that the characterization *distance* is not meant to imply that those who employ this strategy are aloof, standoffish, or distant in their personalities or, at least, that they do not necessarily intend to be so, although they may seem so to some observers (particularly those who prefer a different strategy). The term *distance* refers to the separation that exists between interactants or between speakers and their subject, which results from the application of R1, 'Don't impose'. Such behavior can nonetheless seem quite friendly in interaction with those who expect devices associated with this strategy.

Deference characterizes a style that seems hesitant, since its operating principle is R2, 'Give options'. It governs, for example, the use of euphemisms, which give the interlocutor the choice of not understanding their referent. Use of this principle in interaction may give the impression that the speaker does not know what s/he wants, because s/he is giving the option of decision to the other. However, as with distance, the use of the strategy may be merely conventionalized. Lakoff (1975) points out that women often (and certainly stereotypically) employ this strategy, resulting in the impression that they are fuzzy-minded and indecisive. When asked 'Would you like something to drink?' a person employing a deferent strategy might reply, 'Whatever you're having', or 'Don't go to any trouble'.

Camaraderie conventionalizes equality as an interactive norm and honors the principle R3, 'Be friendly.' This is the strategy typified by the stereotype of the back-slapping American or the car salesman who calls his customers by first names. The person who walks into my house and says, 'I'm thirsty. Do you have any juice?' is employing such a strategy. As with preceding examples, the impression made by such a linguistic choice will depend upon the extent to which I share the expectation that it is appropriate to employ this principle in this situation. My friend may be assuming I will be pleased by the testament to the closeness of our relationship. If I share his/her strategies, I will agree. If not—if I feel, for example, that a little R1 ('Don't impose') might have been nice—then I may get the impression that this person is pushy.

Lakoff's system applies to linguistic choices on all levels. For example, in making lexical choices in talking about sexual activity, technical language such as *copulation* maintains distance between speaker and hearer and between both of them and the emotional content of the subject. It is formal and is appropriate for scientific discussions. Euphemisms such as *doing it* deny not the emotional overtones but the actual subject being referred to; the hearer has the option of not confronting the subject directly. Thus such a choice is associated with a deferent strategy. Finally, the use of colloquial language such as *getting laid* would be appropriate only among equals in informal settings. The association of these various lexical choices with particular settings then yields the possibility of stylistic variation created by usage in other settings. The shared social knowledge of expectation of one register rather than another, in other words, makes it possible to signal metaphorical meaning about the relationship and the situation at hand. For example, the use of colloquial language in a public setting is associated with a particular style: it is a way of communicating the messages, 'I'm just folks', and 'we're all equals'. At the same time, however, such usage of in-group language in a public situation may offend some listeners, those who do not honor camaraderie as the highest goal but would appreciate distance more.

An example of such style shifting is found in a scene in the movie *Georgie Girl*. A woman (Lynn Redgrave) has an affair with her roommate's lover (Alan Bates) while the roommate is in the hospital having Bates' baby. When she discovers that the roommate gave birth just at the time that Redgrave and Bates were in bed together, Redgrave is suddenly repelled by the thought of what they were doing. In talking to him about it, she waves her hand vaguely toward the bedroom and says, 'We were … in there … rolling around'. Her vague gesture, her hesitations, and her use of euphemisms ('in there,' 'rolling around') are all part of what Lakoff terms a deferent style, her use of which, in the context of at-home talk with a lover, serves to dramatize her wish to dissociate herself from what she is talking about. The point is not that she is actually being deferent, but that the use of linguistic devices associated with one setting, when applied in another, has metaphorical significance.

In her later work, Lakoff (1979) envisions the strategies of distance, deference, and camaraderie not as hierarchically ordered but rather as points on a continuum of stylistic preferences. One end of the continuum represents the application of Grice's (1967) maxims, which for her purposes Lakoff refers to as Rules of Clarity. In this style, only the content of the message is important; speakers evidence no involvement with each other or with the subject matter. At the other end of the continuum is camaraderie, governing situations in which the emotional involvement between speakers and between them and their subject matter is maximal.

Each person's decisions about which strategy to apply and to what extent in a given situation results in her/his characteristic style. That style, then, is made up of a range on the continuum, the particular degree of camaraderie or deference, for example, shifting in response to the situation, the people participating, the subject at hand, and so on. Each person's notion of what strategy is appropriate to apply is influenced by a combination of family background and other interactive experience.

As Lakoff points out, unalloyed clarity (a situation governed entirely by Gricean maxims) almost never exists. People prefer not to make themselves perfectly clear because they have interactional goals served by the Rules of Rapport that supersede the goal of clarity (Lakoff 1976). Those higher interactional goals may be broadly subsumed under the headings Defensiveness and Rapport. They correspond, respectively, to a camaraderie strategy and a distance/deference strategy. Thus I may prefer not to let you know just what I mean, so that if you don't like it, I can deny (even to myself) that I meant any such thing. If I don't tell you what I want directly, and you prefer not to give me what I want, I need not feel rejected and you need not feel guilty, because I never really asked for it. This is the defensive benefit of indirectness. On the other hand, if you do give me what I want, how much sweeter (for both of us) if it appears that you gave it to me of your own choice, not because I asked for it. People prefer to feel that they are understood without explaining themselves. Indirectness then can be a testament of love, proof that 'we speak the same language' in the deepest sense. This is the rapport function of indirectness.

A quite separate yet deeply related strand of research in sociology is presented by Goffman, following Durkheim. Durkheim (1915) distinguishes between negative and positive religious rites. Negative rites are religious interdictions, a 'system of abstentions'. However, 'the negative cult is in one sense a means in view of an end: it is a condition of access to the positive cult'. That is, by denying the profane, one prepares for union with the sacred. Goffman (1967) builds on this dichotomy in his notion of deference, 'the appreciation an individual shows of another to that other, whether through avoidance rituals or presentational rituals'. Presentational rituals include 'salutations, invitations, compliments, and minor services. Through all of these the recipient is told that he is not an island unto himself and that others are, or seek to be, involved with him and with his personal private concerns' (pp. 72–73). In contrast, avoidance rituals are 'those forms of deference which lead the actor to keep at a distance from the recipient' (p. 62) and include 'rules regarding privacy and separateness' (p. 67), such as use of polite forms of address, avoidance of certain topics, and so on. (Goffman's concept of 'deference' is not to be confused with Lakoff's but rather corresponds to her more general notion of 'politeness', or 'rapport' as used in 'rules of rapport'.)

Brown and Levinson (1978), building on Lakoff's work on politeness and Goffman's on deference as well as Goffman's (1967) notion of 'face,' identify two aspects of politeness semantics as negative and positive face. Their notion of negative face corresponds to Lakoff's defensive function of indirectness or distance strategy: 'The want of every "competent adult member" that his actions be unimpeded by others'. (Hence Lakoff's operating principle, 'Don't impose'.) Brown and Levinson's notion of positive face corresponds to camaraderie and to the rapport function of indirectness: 'The want of every member that his wants be desirable to at least some others' (p. 67). Negative and positive politeness strategies grow out of these face wants.[2] (One problem with the terms *positive* and *negative* is the possible and certainly unintended value judgments associated with them.) Finally, Brown and Levinson's terms *on record* and *off record* correspond to what has been referred to by others as direct and indirect communication.

Another paradigm that is not precisely parallel but suggests an important corollary to the politeness systems so far discussed is the now classic study by Brown and Gilman (1960) of the dynamics underlying pronoun choice in languages that have both singular (informal) and plural (formal) second person pronouns. Brown and Gilman demonstrate that pronoun choice derives from 'two dimensions fundamental to the analysis of all social life—the dimensions of power and solidarity' (p. 253). Solidarity (associated with reciprocal pronoun use, like Lakoff's suggestion that camaraderie is the strategy of conventionalized equality) is another way of expressing rapport; it is the goal of positive face. Power (associated with nonreciprocal pronoun use, the one in power using the familiar and the other using the polite form) is the

---

[2]A personal anecdote will bring home (literally) the significance of these two face wants. I once had a friend, and a very good friend he was, who asked, before I had read or heard of any of the theories here discussed, what I thought people's greatest drive was. I answered without hesitation, 'the need for community'. He did not agree. He thought it was the need for independence. And so it happened that we did not remain friends. It came about, however, that we met and discussed this same question more than a year later, by which time he had grown rather tired of his single life and I had grown rather fond of mine. I told him that I had come around to his way of thinking: I now agreed that people's greatest drive was to be independent. He told me he had changed his mind as well and decided that I had been right; their greatest need was for community. This eternal back-and-forth seems attributable to the existence of both these basic drives, which we had independently (and in community) hit upon.

dimension the exercise of which provokes defensiveness or negative face.

It has been suggested (Dreyfus 1975; Conley, O'Barr & Lind 1979) that indirectness—the hallmark of Lakoff's deference strategy, Goffman's avoidance rituals, and Brown and Levinson's negative face—is the strategy of choice of those in a position of powerlessness. According to such a hypothesis, this would explain why American women are characteristically more indirect than American men. (Tannen [1981a] provides some evidence that this is so for American men and women but not for Greeks.) Such an analysis is implicit in Lakoff's (1975) pioneering work on language and gender. Dreyfus suggests that indirectness is the only way a subordinate person can manipulate within a relationship without redefining the relationship in a Batesonian sense; that is, direct manipulation would redefine the relationship with the manipulator's power enhanced. These explanations grow out of an understanding of the defensive payoff inherent in indirectness. However, another reason women have been observed to prefer indirectness is that many of them may value more than men the payoff in rapport.

An important point about these two benefits of indirectness is that they are not mutually exclusive. It is not necessary to locate motivations in one and not the other. Moreover, the introduction of the power/solidarity dimension suggests a possible problem in the other theoretical paradigms discussed because they suggest a binary distinction, or polarity, between positive and negative face wants. Lakoff's revised (1979) conceptualization of a continuum rather than a hierarchy of rules is an attempt to correct for this flaw. Indeed, the fact that Brown and Levinson define negative face in negative terms—the need NOT to be imposed on—suggests that negative face is the flip side (like a photographic negative) of positive face rather than a wholly different principle.

A conceptualization that avoids the illusion of polarity is Becker's notion of 'cline of person'. Becker and Oka (1974) claim, 'A central thread—perhaps THE central thread in the semantic structure of all languages is the cline of person, an ordering of linguistic forms according to their distance from the speaker'. The authors continue:

> Between the subjective, pointed, specific pronominal 'I' and the objective, generic common noun, between these poles the words of all languages—words for people, animals, food, time, space, indeed words for everything—are ordered and categorized according to their distance—spatial, temporal, social, biological, and metaphorical—from the first person, the speaker. The cline of person also underlies most linguistic systems as well

as words, systems of deixis, number, definiteness, tense, and nominal classification among others. (p. 229)

Another such linguistic system is that of stylistic strategies under discussion here.

Put another way, human beings are always balancing the paradoxical fact that they are simultaneously individuals and social creatures. They need each other and yet they need to be separate. This conflict can be seen in what I think of as the paradox of cross-cultural communication. Individuals of any minority or special interest group can be heard to protest, alternately, 'Don't assume I'm different from you', and 'Don't assume I'm the same as you'. Assuming some people are different leads to discrimination and even persecution. But assuming everyone is the same effectively locks out those who actually are different in some ways—another form of discrimination. Hence, affirmative action. It is not that members of minority groups want to eat their cakes and have them too, but that we are all caught in the double bind of being the same and not the same as others. That is why all communication is a double bind, as Scollon (1982:344) points out, in the sense that participants receive and send 'a double and contradictory message, and a bonding that makes it difficult to leave the situation'. Scollon observes, too, and this I think is crucial, that it is not that each message must service either one or the other need, but that 'any message must be a carefully concocted blend of the right amounts of deference and solidarity'.

A final related strand of research that reflects the cline of person as an influence on discourse form is a broad range of discourse features that have been identified as characterizing spoken or written language, respectively. Such features, which are summarized and discussed elsewhere (Tannen 1982; in press-a) include such phenomena as complexity of syntactic structure, discourse organization, degree of elaboration or ellipsis of necessary background information, and a variety of features that Chafe (1982) has grouped under the headings integration vs. fragmentation and detachment vs. involvement. I have suggested that these various features of discourse reflect not the spoken vs. written modes per se but rather relative focus on interpersonal involvement. That is, the features that we have come to expect and that scholars have identified in spoken language (for example, prolixity; use of intonational cues to express attitudes and establish cohesion rather than complex syntactic structures; indirectness and omission of contextual and background information) all grow out of and contribute to interpersonal involvement between the speaker (or writer) and the audience. By leaving maximal information for the hearer to fill in, a speaker is creating involvement by requiring the hearer to participate in sensemaking.

There are complementary discourse features that have been identified in written language but in fact are most often found in the specific written genre of expository prose. Those features seem to focus on content, for example, filling in maximal steps of an argument and background information, and making use of complex syntactic structures to lexicalize cohesive relationships. This focus on content, which is also associated with spoken language in formal or nondialogic genres, also conspires to ignore interpersonal involvement, a way of honoring participants' needs to avoid the negative effects of involvement.

A final way to approach this very basic dimension is to consider the positive and negative aspects of closeness. In the original version of the present book, I repeatedly discussed the styles of participants in terms that assumed closeness to be a positive value. Ron Scollon, drawing on his experience among Athabaskan Indians in Alaska, repeatedly reminded me that for some, closeness is a danger, not a goal. Acknowledging the possible ethnocentricity in my instinctive feeling that talk is a way of expressing and establishing rapport, I tried to be open-minded and corrected my analysis to allow that two people could feel close because they talk to each other a lot or because they are comfortable with silence. Scollon noted, correctly, that I was still assuming that closeness has an inherent positive value. He quoted a Tlingit (native Alaskan) woman who said something to the effect that 'when two people get close, it is important for them to seek out the neat things about each other to prevent the development of the hostility that people feel when they are close'. This reflects an assumption that closeness has an inherent negative value because it entails hostility.

A similar assumption, or rather hypothesis, has been suggested by Pask (1980), who maintains that too much togetherness inhibits conversation (*conversation* here is used as a technical term denoting information transfer in which concepts are actually shared).

In this, human beings are like Bettelheim's (1979:204) image, borrowed from Schopenhauer, of two porcupines trying to get through a cold winter. They huddle together for warmth but find that their sharp quills prick each other, so they pull away and get cold. They have to keep adjusting their closeness and distance in order to survive the cold and the quills.[3] What we have, then, is a paradoxical situation regarding

---

[3] I am grateful to Pamela Gerloff for sending me this reference.

the need for and dangers of interpersonal involvement, such that it entails both positive and negative values that are balanced, honored, and valued differently in different linguistic and cultural systems. Every act of communication must somehow serve these dual and conflicting needs, according to the constraints furnished by a speaker's communicative style.

Processes of Conversational Style

Conversational style, then, results from the need to serve basic human needs in interaction. Similarly, the linguistic strategies that make up conversational style do not exist in a vacuum but arise in response to the strategies used by the others in the interaction.

Lakoff (1978) shows that the basic transformational functions (addition, subtraction, deletion, and permutation) operate in personality as in language. For example, she points out that the psychological process of repression is a form of deletion by which an element present in underlying structure does not appear in surface structure. The psychoanalytic process of reaction formation corresponds to substitution; an element present in underlying structure appears in a different form in surface structure. Through these processes, Lakoff demonstrates, verbal strategies exhibit *ambiguity* and *paraphrase* functions. Just as one sentence may have two different deep structures (e.g. Visiting relatives can be a nuisance), so behavior can be ambiguous. I may continually flick my hand across my face because there is an elusive strand of hair in my eyes or because I have an obsessive delusion that there is something obstructing my vision. Similarly, just as two different sentences may have the same deep structure (e.g. active and passive forms), so behavior can be paraphrastic. Feelings of insecurity can be expressed by habitually putting oneself down or by habitually putting others down. (Examples are my own.)

These basic grammatical relations, then, function in conversation and contribute to the dissonance that prevails in interaction between speakers with differing styles. This process has been analyzed in detail in the dialogue from Ingmar Bergman's *Scenes from a Marriage* (Lakoff and Tannen in press). Pragmatic synonymy (paraphrase) can be seen in the way the husband, Johan, and the wife, Marianne, use different linguistic devices to achieve similar ends. In order to avoid unpleasant topics (for example, their marital problems), Marianne characteristically uses excessive verbiage about trifling details or a barrage of questions, both associated with a camaraderie strategy. Johan employs the distancing strategies of sarcasm, pontification, and pompousness. Pragmatic homonymy (ambiguity) is the phenomenon by which they use the same linguistic devices to achieve different ends. For example, Johan and Marianne both employ rhetorical questions. However, Marianne's questions attempt to draw Johan into her idealized vision of how their life should be, whereas Johan's function as taunts to drive her away.

Whenever a speaker in interaction uses a device that the interlocutor understands as intended, a situation of pragmatic identity exists. This is the ideal, the goal, of communication. However, in as many cases— perhaps more often than we would like to believe—misunderstandings arise as a result of pragmatic homonymy and synonymy. (The distinction between understanding and misunderstanding is an idealized one. In actual interaction, speakers and listeners achieve varying degrees of understanding of each other's intentions. That is, a listener may form an impression that corresponds more or less closely to the model the speaker is operating from. It is probably the case that precise fits—the experience of having one's listener perceive precisely what one intends, with all its associations, connotations, and overtones—are relatively rare, if not impossible, and that complete misunderstandings—the experience of having one's listener perceive quite the opposite of one's intentions or something utterly unrelated to one's intentions—are equally rare.)

An example of pragmatic homonymy can be seen in the following example. A first-year graduate student (Mary) arrived at a meeting attended mostly by experienced graduate students. While waiting for the meeting to begin, Mary introduced herself to the others present. When one of the other students, Sue, told Mary her full name, her fellow students remarked on the fact that she had given a new last name. Mary asked Sue whether the name change was the result of marriage or divorce. On hearing that Sue had gotten divorced, Mary offered the information that she herself was recently divorced and had recently resumed use of her family name. She then asked Sue a series of questions, such as when she had gotten divorced, how long she had been married, and so on. Years later, Mary had occasion to learn that Sue had been offended by her barrage of personal questions, which she had taken not as an expression of interest but as imposing, intrusive, and overbearing. Mary had been operating on a camaraderie strategy, seeking to make herself and her new acquaintance feel good by behaving as if they were friends and could talk freely about their common personal experiences. Sue, however, expected Lakoff's R1 to apply (Don't impose), so Mary's approach did not make her feel good at all. She concluded not that Mary was friendly but that she was nosy. In other words, a situation of pragmatic homonymy prevailed by which the verbal device of offering and asking for personal information had different meanings for speaker and hearer.[4]

An example of pragmatic synonymy has been presented and analyzed (though not in these terms) in Gumperz and Tannen 1979.[5] The conversation took place between close friends as one was preparing dinner for them both. Readers will be interested in knowing that one of these speakers, the one called Steve, is also a participant in the Thanksgiving dinner conversation:

(1)   John: What kind of salad dressing should I make?

(2)   Steve: Oil and vinegar, what else?

(3)   John: What do you mean, 'What else?'

(4)   Steve: Well, I always make oil and vinegar, but if you want we could try something else.

(5)   John: Does that mean you don't like it when I make other dressings?

(6)   Steve: No. I like it. Go ahead. Make something else.

(7)   John: Not if you want oil and vinegar.

(8)   Steve: I don't. Make a yogurt dressing.

(John prepares yogurt dressing, tastes it, and makes a face.)

(9)   Steve: Isn't it good?

(10)   John: I don't know how to make yogurt dressing.

(11)   Steve: Well if you don't like it, throw it out.

(12)   John: Never mind.

(13)   Steve: What never mind? It's just a little yogurt!

(14)   John: You're making a big deal about nothing!

(15)   Steve: YOU are!

---

[4]The development of this relationship is a case in point of the possible effects of awareness of style differences. For a period, the two women met regularly in the university setting and found each other's behavior distressing. Mary was often hurt by what she perceived as Sue's aloofness, and she continued to offend Sue by her unwitting intrusiveness. After a while, however, the two got to know each other and had occasion to discuss their style differences. They grew to like each other and enjoy each other's company at school. They did not, however, seek each other's company in social settings. The knowledge that a person is using a different strategy may make her style comprehensible, but not necessarily enjoyable.

[5]This conversation was not tape-recorded but reported to me later that evening by both speakers together. Slight changes in wording from the form presented in Gumperz and Tannen 1979 reflect the participants' later adjustments, after having seen the conversation in print, but those changes are minor and do not affect the dynamics.

This interchange resulted in both speakers feeling that the other was being uncooperative and difficult. Discussion of the incident with both parties after the fact revealed that when John asked (1) 'What kind of salad dressing should I make?' he expected Steve to say something like, 'Make whatever you want', or, at most, a general suggestion like, 'Why not make something creamy?' In other words, John expected a strategy that was careful not to impose, as he was doing when he asked (1) instead of just preparing something he liked. The use of such verbal devices associated with one strategy or another is conventionalized. A speaker does not consciously refer to the operating principles but simply speaks in ways that seem obviously appropriate.

Expecting, therefore, to be given the option of what salad dressing to prepare, or at least a negotiation ('Make something creamy'), John was thrown off balance by Steve's reply (2) 'Oil and vinegar, what else?' Yet Steve later explained that his reply meant precisely 'Make whatever you want'. He intended 'what else' as a self-mocking ironic comment on his own unimaginative eating habits, implying therefore that it would be best for John to decide what kind of dressing to make. It might be paraphrased as, 'Well if you ask me I'm going to say oil and vinegar because I'm so dull, that's what I always make; since you're more imaginative, why don't you make whatever you like'. The situation is one of pragmatic synonymy: different ways of saying what amounts to the same thing.

The yogurt dressing example also illustrates the phenomenon Bateson (1972) has identified and dubbed 'complementary schismogenesis'. This is a dynamic in which two interactants exercise clashing behavior, such that each one's behavior drives the other into increasingly exaggerated expressions of the incongruent behavior in a mutually aggravating spiral. A classic example is that of a couple, one partner of which tends to exhibit dependent behavior, while the other tends toward independent behavior. The dependent partner tends to cling out of fear of losing the other. This clinging aggravates the independent partner's claustrophobia and incites him/her to seek more independence. The resulting drawing away gives evidence to the other partner that s/he had better cling more tightly lest the other drift further away, and so on, in an ever widening gyre. (Note that the process does not necessarily begin with the behavior of one or the other partner but is a spontaneous outgrowth of their mutual behavior.) Watzlawick, Beavin, and Jackson (1967) give numerous examples of this dynamic in interaction.

In the yogurt dressing example, one speaker, John, becomes increasingly adamant in his determination to honor Steve's preferences, and, consequently, in his conviction that Steve is bossing him around, as he sees expressions of Steve's preferences in his speech. Steve, on the other hand, tries harder and harder to convince John that he is not expressing his preferences at all, with the paradoxical result that he appears more and more demanding. He goes from the ironic 'what else' (2) to a suggestion 'we could try something else' (4) to a general imperative 'Make something else (6) to a specific imperative 'Make a yogurt dressing' (8). This last was intended as proof of good faith, to make it abundantly clear that he is willing to eat any kind of dressing. In other words, 'yogurt dressing' stands for *something other than oil and vinegar*. John, however, takes it literally, as a demand for yogurt dressing.[6] Thus John and Steve were caught in the grip of pragmatic synonyms.

Frames and How they are Signaled

Another process identified by Bateson that can be seen in the yogurt dressing example is that of frames. Bateson (1972) shows that no message can be interpreted except by reference to a superordinate message about how the communication is intended. *Play,* for example, is a frame within which a bite or a slap is not hostile. The metamessage *this is play* signals the context within which a bite or a slap does not stand for what it is known to mean, namely, aggression.

Thus, the way that Steve said, 'Oil and vinegar, what else?' signaled the frame, irony, by which it was not intended to mean what it would otherwise have meant, i.e., You're a dolt for asking. The metamessage *This is irony* is cued by a combination of intonation, voice quality, facial expression, gesture, plus the expectation that such usage is appropriate to the situation. These subtle signals are opaque, however, to John or to anyone unfamiliar with this brand of irony.

The notion of frame as a category within which meaning must be interpreted is parallel to concepts in philosophy of language. Van Valin (1977) explains that Wittgenstein's notion of meaning as use entails that there can be no purely referential meaning. Wittgenstein, for example,

---

[6]To suggest that John did not understand how Steve intended his remark is not to deny the validity of John's response to it. From John's point of view, Steve's use of irony in this context was inappropriate and hurtful. John is not likely to change his emotional reaction to such a usage, but both he and Steve are better off if he understands that Steve did not intend to be hurtful.

pointed out that the word *hammer* can have no meaning to someone unfamiliar with how a hammer is used. This amounts, in effect, to a *frames* approach to semantics (Fillmore 1976). The name *hammer,* like the object it names, can be understood only by reference to a frame or set of expectations about human behavior which includes the use of a hammer. This insight is substantiated over and over in ethnography of speaking research. For example, Agar (1975) shows that it is impossible to understand the language used by street junkies unless one understands the experiences that give rise to it.

However, the question remains for linguists of how the dynamic notion of frames operates in language, given an interactional model of speech events.[7] The interface between macro sociolinguistic theory and micro linguistic analysis is to be found in the work of John Gumperz and his associates.

Gumperz (1977, 1982b) demonstrates that speakers signal what activity they are engaging in, i.e. the metacommunicative frame they are operating within, by use of paralinguistic and prosodic features of speech such as intonation, pitch, amplitude, rhythm, and so on. Gumperz calls these features, when they are used to signal interpretive frames (in his terms, 'speech activities'), 'contextualization cues.'

Adopting a cross-cultural perspective, Gumperz has developed a method for investigating the operation of contextualization cues by examining situations in which they fail to work: situations of culture contact in which participants interact with others who do not share their conventions for signaling meaning. At the same time that the culture contact situation provides the theoretician with a heuristic device for analyzing the operation of contextualization cues, the theory provides a way of understanding the breakdown of communication that occurs in such situations. In other words, in addition to addressing the theoretical question about the nature of social knowledge in language use, the method also offers an invaluable tool in the understanding of practical and ubiquitous social problems arising out of culture contact situations such as are found in modern urban environments.

Gumperz' method involves isolating the operation of contextualization cues by comparing conversational interaction among in-group

---

[7]The key work on frames is Goffman (1974). Frake (1977) cautions that frames are dynamic and ever changing, not static. Tannen (1979) discusses the term as related to other concepts in a variety of fields, and Tannen (in press-b) and Tannen and Wallat (1983) demonstrate how the notion of frame sheds light on communication in a pediatric setting.

members with cross-cultural interaction. One example Gumperz (1978a) discusses at length is a public address in which a black activist alienated his primarily white audience and got himself arrested for threatening the life of the United States president. At a rally at the University of California, Berkeley, the speaker repeatedly intoned, 'We will kill Richard Nixon'. Gumperz shows that the speaker was using rhetorical devices of black preaching style as well as a black colloquialism, 'kill', to convey the meaning of destroying Nixon's influence, not his life. Had the intended meaning been to assassinate the president, the appropriate colloquialism would have been 'waste', or another metaphorical term. The rhetorical strategies employed in this speech are shown to operate in an example of black preaching taped from a radio broadcast, and interviews with members of the black community testify to the fact that in-group members made the same interpretation that the speaker later professed to have meant.

Gumperz has done considerable research, as well, in comparing the contextualization systems of speakers of Indian English with those of speakers of British and American English. He shows that speakers of Indian English consistently have trouble getting their ideas listened to and appreciated in conversations with speakers of British or American English. In one study Gumperz (1978b) reports on research in an on-the-job culture contact situation that shows how contextualization cues operate. Indian women newly hired to serve meals to employees at a London airport cafeteria were considered surly and uncooperative by both customers and supervisors. The employees themselves felt that they were being mistreated and discriminated against. Taperecording interaction and playing it back in a workshop setting revealed that use of intonation and prosody was playing a large part in the trouble. For example, when offering gravy to customers who had chosen meat, the Indian women said, 'Gravy'. Their falling intonation was quite different from the rising intonation with which British women, when serving, offered, 'Gravy?' Listening to the tapes in mixed groups of Indian and British employees, the Indian women expressed their feeling that they were saying the same thing and could not account for the negative reaction they were getting. The British women then pointed out that the different intonation patterns yield different meanings. Whereas the question, 'Gravy?' uttered with rising intonation is understood to mean, *Would you like gravy?* the same word uttered with falling intonation sounds like a statement and is understood to mean, *This is gravy. Take it or leave it.*

In this way Gumperz' approach accounts, in part, for what may otherwise be ascribed to prejudice or discrimination, but may, in fact, be attributable to the systematic misjudgment of the intentions and abilities of those from other cultures or subcultures who employ contextualization cues in different ways. This is not to adopt the polyanna stance that discrimination and prejudice do not exist but simply to note that they are aggravated by concrete differences in language use.

The degree to which cultural background is shared is reflected, then, in the degree to which use of contextualization cues is congruent, that is, whether speakers can gauge when others have made their points, when interruption is appropriate, what interactive frame is operative, what the relationship is between comments. Members of similar cultures but different subcultures may be able to manage these conversational control mechanisms, but yet misunderstand each other's uses of such devices as irony and indirectness, as seen in the yogurt dressing example. (See Gumperz and Tannen 1979 for further discussion of this phenomenon.)

The ability to participate appropriately in a discussion of any sort depends upon the ability to signal and comprehend the relations between elements within utterances and across utterances, in other words to tell what someone else's main points are as distinguished from background material and to make clear one's own main points and their relations to background material. Put another way, speakers must maintain *thematic progression* (Bennett 1978b). The crucial nature of this ability can be sensed from the feeling of discomfort that arises when you cannot tell what someone else is getting at, and, therefore, you cannot determine what your response should be. Keenan and Schieffelin (1975) discuss this phenomenon in conversation as the ability to maintain *topic*. Their notion of topic corresponds to Bennett's thematic progression. In fact, it is thematic progression that is at issue in many linguistics papers dealing with topic as a syntactic phenomenon, as well as in recent studies of cohesion (for example, Halliday and Hasan 1976). The crucial distinctions made by Chafe (1974) between given and new information and between new information and contrastiveness, are also concerned with this matter of tying things together and cuing the relationship among elements within uttered material.

Michaels and Cook-Gumperz (1979) illustrate what can happen when thematic progression in narratives is signaled differently by members of interacting groups. They have studied narratives told by black and white children in a first grade classroom in Berkeley, California. The teacher expects a *topic-centered* narrative strategy that corresponds to the strategy employed by white children in the class. Hence she is able to identify their talk as narrative and understand the point of their stories. In contrast, the black children employ a *topic-chaining* strategy with which the teacher is unfamiliar. Therefore, she does not recognize their talk as narrative; rather she gets the impression that the children are just rambling, and she cuts them off before they make their points. The black children use intonation to cue topic shifts within their talk, but like the contextualization cues used to signal irony in the yogurt dressing example discussed earlier, the signals of topic shift in the black children's talk are lost on the teacher who is unfamiliar with the devices. In this setting, the results of differences in ways of building and signaling thematic progression can be tragic indeed.

Conversational Styles in Interaction

These research paradigms and examples furnish a theoretical basis for understanding conversational style, that is, ways of signaling how any utterance is meant. The system of cues is not random. Rather it is made up of devices based on strategies for serving the simultaneous and conflicting need for and danger of interpersonal involvement. Whenever style is shared, there is a metamessage of rapport. The fact that people understand each other's ways of signaling meaning is in itself proof of shared background and context. The implication is not that speakers necessarily or consciously attempt to invoke solidarity when they speak, although that may be the case, more or less consciously, when a recognizably in-group style or code is used. (Blom and Gumperz [1972] identify this phenomenon as metaphorical code-switching.) Rather, habitual ways of talking make use of verbal devices that honor rapport and considerateness in conventionalized ways. Because of the paradoxical nature of closeness (and consequently of communication), speakers must constantly observe both the need for involvement and the need not to impose, or, expressed positively, for considerateness.

The involvement/considerateness dimension sheds light on much recent research, including my own (Tannen 1980) on Greek and American oral narrative style. In my study, I found that many of the features Greek speakers used in telling what happened in a film they had seen could be understood as serving the goal of telling good stories. For example, they used details to support an interpretation of the film's message, they were comparatively free in their interpretation of events, and they judged the behavior of the characters in the film. These and other features highlighted the interpersonal involvement between the speakers and their audience. In contrast, the Americans in the study seemed to be performing a memory task, including more details and emphasizing temporal order for the sake of accuracy. In this, they conventionally ignored the involvement of the audience and tried to perform an objective task.

In another cross-cultural study (Tannen 1981a) I compared strategies used by Greek and American informants in interpreting a short conversation:

(1)   Wife: John's having a party. Wanna go?

(2)   Husband: OK.

(3)   Wife: (later) Are you sure you want to go?

(4)   Husband: OK, let's not go. I'm tired anyway.

In choosing variant interpretations, more Greeks than Americans favored the interpretation that the husband's response (2) 'OK' did not mean that he really wanted to go to the party. Rather, they believed that he was going along with what he perceived as his wife's indirect indication in (1) that she wanted to go. The reason most often given by Greek respondents to explain why they made this interpretation, was the husband's lack of enthusiasm in his response 'OK'. This finding corresponds to results of quite a different kind of study by Vassiliou, Triandis, Vassiliou, and McGuire (1972) to the effect that Greeks place more value on enthusiasm and spontaneity than do Americans.

Related to this enthusiasm constraint is another phenomenon that I dubbed the 'brevity effect'. In explaining why they made certain interpretations, many respondents in both groups referred to the brevity of the husband's (2) 'OK'. However, all Americans who made reference to the brevity of 'OK', did so to explain why they believed the husband really wanted to go to the party. They reasoned that the brevity of his response showed that he was being casual, informal, and hence sincere. This interpretation is based on the assumption that, in an in-group setting, one will say just what s/he means. In stark contrast, Greeks who mentioned the brevity of the husband's 'OK' did so in support of the interpretation that he did not really want to go to the party. Their interpretation was based on the assumption that, in an in-group setting, resistance to the other's will should not be expressed directly, so it will be expressed by saying little. The strategy is a variation of the adage, If you can't say something good, don't say anything.

Thus for the in-group setting posed, the Greek speakers in my study evidenced a communicative strategy by which enthusiasm was expected in a sincere expression of one's preferences, and brevity was expected in expression of unwillingness to comply with the perceived wish of a close partner. The American respondents revealed less expectation of enthusiasm and stated that brevity was associated with the direct communication of one's preferences. In the first system, the signaling load was on interpersonal solidarity through expression of enthusiasm. In the second system the signaling load was on the content, which is, therefore, taken at face value.

Moreover, in interviews in which respondents discussed why they chose one or the other interpretation, Greek subjects more often personalized their analyses. That is, they reported having made interpretations by reference to their own experience, saying things like, 'Well, that's how my husband does it', or, 'If I were the one . . .' Americans, on the other hand, were more likely to try to be objective in their analyses. As with the narratives told by Greek women in the film experiment, the Greek approach is more personalized and exhibits strategies associated with social interaction rather than the depersonalized approaches used by American respondents that are associated with formal schooling (as observed by Goody and Watt 1963 and Olson 1977).

The findings of other researchers can also be understood in terms of relative focus on involvement. For example, Courtney Cazden and Frederick Erickson have directed research on communicative strategies in bilingual classrooms. Their initial research indicated that not only Anglo-American teachers but even Chicano teachers praised Anglo-American children more than Chicano children in mixed classrooms. Research assistants Arthur Vera and Robert Carrasco began to take part in Chicago bilingual classrooms and thereby discovered that what was going on was more subtle than was suspected at first.

Although they did not praise Chicano children publicly, the Chicano teachers found opportunities to praise them in private. At those times they also thanked them for having performed well for the benefit of the teacher. This contrasts strikingly with what has been observed by Sarah Michaels (personal communication) in her role as participant-observer in an ethnically mixed elementary school in California (in connection with a project directed by John Gumperz and Herb Simons). Michaels notes that the white teacher in her classroom praised children publicly for their performance and regularly reminded them that they were performing not for her but for themselves.

The white and Chicano teachers in these studies used strategies resulting in different teaching styles which are consistent with the involvement/considerateness distinction. By refraining from singling children out for public praise, the Chicano teacher honors the importance of the children's mutual solidarity. The motivation of pleasing the teacher encourages the child to perform well in school, based on the interpersonal connection between the child and the teacher. In contrast, the Anglo-American teacher's strategy of public praise is likely to engender competitiveness in children. Such competitiveness is indeed observed in Michaels' study and not in the Chicano teachers' classrooms. Furthermore, the Anglo-American teacher's deemphasis of her personal connection with the children leads her to urge them to perform for their own sakes. In striking contrast, the Chicano teacher, when praising Chicano children, regularly takes them into her lap, caresses them affectionately, and calls them endearing pet names—all devices associated with a family, in-group rapport system.

Features of High-involvement Style

The issues of how and how much interpersonal involvement is overtly signaled lie at the heart of the analysis of conversational style that constitutes the present study. It will be shown that the devices used by certain speakers in the extended conversation analyzed can be seen as conventionalized ways of establishing rapport by honoring the needs for involvement and for considerateness.

The features used in devices that put the signaling load on interpersonal involvement, all of which are defined, demonstrated, and discussed in subsequent chapters, include:

1. Topic
   a. Prefer personal topics
   b. Shift topics abruptly
   c. Introduce topics without hesitance
   d. Persistence (if a new topic is not immediately picked up, reintroduce it, repeatedly if necessary)
2. Pacing
   a. Faster rate of speech
   b. Faster turn taking
   c. Avoid interturn pauses (silence shows lack of rapport)
   d. Cooperative overlap
   e. Participatory listenership

3. Narrative strategies
   a. Tell more stories
   b. Tell stories in rounds
   c. Prefer internal evaluation (i.e. point of a story is dramatized rather than lexicalized)
4. Expressive paralinguistics
   a. Expressive phonology
   b. Marked pitch and amplitude shifts
   c. Marked voice quality
   d. Strategic within-turn pauses

These features are not randomly distributed in the speech of the speakers studied. Though no two speakers use all the same devices in the same way, there are patterns by which these devices co-occur in the speech of certain participants. The combination of particular devices makes up the style of each speaker. The broad operating principles by which particular devices are used for particular effects are conversational strategies.

To the extent they were used, these and other features were combined in differing combinations in the speech of three speakers at Thanksgiving dinner. Use of these features enhanced conversational flow when used among these three speakers but obstructed conversational flow when used with the other three speakers. Comments by all participants upon listening to the conversation on tape indicated that the other three misinterpreted or misjudged the intentions of speakers who used these devices, and the speakers who used them were puzzled by the others' behavior, which they interpreted as autonomous expressions of character and intentions, not as reactions to their own conversational styles.

All of these features can be understood as expressing (in the terms of John Gumperz, putting the signaling load on) involvement, or rapport. Hence, I shall refer to the speakers who use them as exhibiting a high-involvement style. In contrast, the other three speakers expected and used strategies that expressed (or put the signaling load on) the need not to impose. Hence, I shall refer to these speakers as using a high-considerateness style.

All speakers were trying to observe both the need for rapport and the need for considerateness in ways that seemed self-evidently appropriate; they were simply having conversation. However, the ways that seemed natural to do this were different for each; one group saw fit to show involvement (or solidarity, or rapport) and the other saw fit to show considerateness, in different degrees and in different ways.

Procedure and Analytic Method

The identification of the listed features and their operation in interaction, which will be demonstrated in the following analysis, is based on the conversation recorded at a Thanksgiving dinner at which I was a guest. It will be helpful to explain a little about how I went about the recording as well as some problems I see in this procedure.

Shortly after everyone had arrived, I asked for permission to tape the conversation. Everyone there knew of my interest in studying conversation, so no one was surprised, but no one knew beforehand that I would record this conversation. Reactions ranged from that of the participants Steve and Peter, who I believe were flattered and enjoyed the opportunity to be taped, to that of Chad, who I believe was genuinely put off a bit because of his reticence about being taped in general and the fact that he was a newcomer to the group. (After getting to know the styles of these speakers in the analysis, readers will see that their attitudes toward being taped are consonant with other components of their styles. It is a problem inherent in studying conversation that some people's styles lead them to be more comfortable, even eager, about being taperecorded than others.) I had no specific intention, at that point, to base my dissertation on this recording. I was in the habit, at that time, of carrying my tape recorder with me everywhere and turning it on whenever people did not mind.

On this occasion, everyone consented, and I placed the tape recorder in the middle of the rectangular table. The tape recorder used was a Sony TC150, a small (7 in. × 4-$\frac{1}{2}$ in.) recorder in a black leather case. Only the internal microphone was used, sacrificing quality of recording to minimize the intrusiveness of the machine. Recording began before the dinner, so that at the beginning some people were walking around, preparing, while I sat, with various others, at the table.

I had brought a 120-minute cassette, so two one-hour segments were recorded without interruption. At the end of the two hours, the tape recorder sat idle for a time. Somewhat later, participants noticed that the tape recorder had stopped, just as they had previously noticed that it was still running. They regretted (as I did) that I had not brought another blank tape, so the host produced a 60-minute cassette, and another 40 minutes of conversation was recorded. In the interim between tapes, a seventh participant arrived who is deaf and does not speak. Therefore, he was not recorded (although his presence clearly influenced the interaction), so his style could not be analyzed. (Although he became the focus of attention later in the evening, during the 40 minutes of taping at which he was present this was not the case.)

The fact that I was a participant in the conversation entails advantages and disadvantages for analysis. An important aspect of both is that it affords analysis of a special and crucial kind of communication: talk among friends. Because some of the participants knew each other well and had histories and connections among them, meaning constructed in their talk is perhaps a bit harder for a conversational analyst to grasp, because the meaning does not reside only in the immediate conversation but has been created over time. However, difficulty for the analyst is not sufficient reason to avoid a crucial aspect of human behavior. Recording a conversation among friends that would have taken place anyway makes available for study patterns of language use that do not emerge among strangers, such as playful routines, irony and allusion, reference to familiar jokes and assumptions. People who regularly interact with each other create a special language between and among them, a language that is called upon and built upon in their continuing interactions (and dies when they cease to interact, which is part of the pain of severing relationships).

In order to confront head-on the issue of objectivity and possible bias, and to keep both the dangers and the benefits of my involvement in the readers' minds as well as my own, I have written this book in the first person. It seems to me that referring to oneself as data in the third person (e.g., B says X, where the speaker objectively referred to as B is none other than the writer's own beloved self), is to invoke a deceptive objectivity. Referring to oneself as participant as well as analyst (e.g., I said X) may be initially jarring to the reader accustomed to objective-sounding academic prose, but it is more honest with respect to both the subjectivity of the writer and the writer's special insight into the motivations and on-the-spot experience of at least one participant.

Two Issues in Analyzing Recorded Conversation

There is a paradox inherent in recording conversation for analysis (as Charles Fillmore points out) if one is committed both to collecting natural data and securing the informed consent of participants. So long as participants are aware of the presence of the tape recorder, their talk is not natural. No problem, say the sociolinguists. If there is a relatively large number of participants who have ongoing social relationships, they soon forget the tape recorder. People play to the crowd (Blom and Gumperz 1972; Labov 1972). It is clear that this happened in my study. On the four occasions when people noticed and remarked on the taping, the quality of their surprise (for example, 'Are you still taping?!') is evidence that they had forgotten about it. But if they forgot they were being taped, was their consent not effectively canceled?

In order to overcome this problem, consent is again sought after the taping. Each participant in my study listened to the tape afterwards and again consented to my use of it. They also read the complete analysis and once more consented to publication (with names changed). What is more difficult, however, is the question of how informed their consent could be, that is, whether they could have anticipated the impact of microanalysis.

By capturing the speech of this interaction on tape, I irrevocably altered the experience for those who participated. By asking them to listen to the interaction after the fact, I confronted them with images of themselves which, like it or not, have remained with them. By discussing with them and with their friends their conversational styles and the impact of their styles on the group interaction, I created an awareness in them and in their friends that cannot be erased, even if they had asked that the tape be erased and I had complied. Views of their styles, and their interacting styles, as I interpreted them, have continued to be the topic of thought and conversation among the speakers, all of whom have remained friends. Some have said they have found the insights helpful. This is a great relief to me, for I am sure they were not always pleasurable, since both of the above also apply to me as a participant.

It is a problem, not only for participants, but also for the analyst and for readers who wish to put the present study in perspective, that the process of microanalysis leads to distortion as well as insight. (This phenomenon has been discussed by Pittenger et al. 1960 and Labov and Fanshel 1977.) Capturing a person's speech for analysis necessarily creates an image of that person and her/his behavior that is out of proportion to the impact they might have had in actual interaction. Everyone has had the experience of wincing on seeing her/himself captured in a photograph; one's nose looks too long, one's cheeks look hollow, one has been trapped in a grimace. It is not that the expression reported by the camera is not true (the camera can only reflect what entered its lens). But the capturing for all time what was a fleeting moment within a stream of behavior necessarily falsifies the essential nature of the glance. Similarly, any person's speech can be rendered absurd, comic, bizarre, or foolish, if it is wrenched out of context and held up for analysis. However, if it is not wrenched out of context, it cannot be analyzed. This paradox is operative in the present study. I believe my analysis is true to one angle of the picture, but I must remind my readers (and myself) that it is one angle only. At the same time that what I say about the interaction is true, there are also many other truths; had the photograph been snapped a second later, the nose might have looked shorter and the cheeks less hollow, though they would be, nonetheless, the same nose and cheeks composing the same face.

As soon as conversation is recorded on tape, it becomes a new entity—a taped conversation—that is different from the conversation as it occurred. For one thing, as has been pointed out, a recording is fixed in time and available for precise reproduction, whereas the very essence of talk is that it disappears as soon as it is uttered and can be imperfectly reconstructed but not retrieved. In addition, the talk as uttered in the actual interaction is one channel of an integrated complex including nonverbal components such as facial expression, body movement, gesture, and so on. To isolate the verbal channel necessarily distorts the picture. In some cases, the loss of the other channels renders talk incomprehensible. Sometimes meaning can be reconstructed by reference to memory, if not one's own, then perhaps that of another member of the group, or by retrieval of physical objects that were present at the time. Thus, for example, at two points in the Thanksgiving conversation, talk referred to a promotional flyer advertising a recital that one of the participants would be performing in. The first time I listened to the tape, this segment made little sense to me. After playing it for others who had been present, however, I was reminded that we had been discussing the flyer, and the one whose performance it announced was able to send me a copy of it, making comprehensible numerous details of our comments that would otherwise have remained opaque.

Despite the exercise of memory and retrieval of objects, however, there are necessarily segments that will make little sense, and those that seem to make perfect sense may nonetheless appear different than they did at the time. Again, what the tape recorder picks up was necessarily there, but it can only pick up a piece of the interaction, and no piece can be completely understood without the whole of which it was a part.

The tape recorder distorts, too, in that it picks up what is nearest to it. Some voices record more easily than others; some speakers were sitting closer to the recorder. One participant, Sally, spoke very softly, and, therefore, some of her speech was inaudible. Unfortunately, she was also comparatively far from the recorder. In addition, there were numerous overlapping conversations. At the time, each participant listened to only one of those conversations. As observers, we want to hear both. In some cases it was possible through focused and repeated listening to decipher both parallel conversations; in others cases the overlapping talk made one or both incomprehensible.

Finally, the tape recorder remained stable, while the people moved. Therefore, those who remained in the room with the recorder had more of their speech recorded than did those who occasionally moved into the kitchen. (I remained seated near the recorder the entire time, and this obviously played a role in the fact that I made the greatest number of recorded contributions.)

As one catalogues the weaknesses of the tape recorded conversation to reflect the interaction that occurred, the endeavor can begin to seem nearly hopeless. However, the other side of the coin is this: on the basis of the recording, we can retrieve much of the material that was a crucial part of the interaction, and when listening to the recording the participants retrieved a very large part of the experience that remained dormant in their memories. Furthermore, the isolation of a single channel is not so dreadful a shortcoming in light of the redundancy of channels. Information lost from nonverbal channels, such as facial expressions, gestures, and body movements, is rarely totally different from that preserved in the speech channel. Rather, it reinforces the messages communicated through language.

In order to study the taped conversation, we must take it yet another step from actual interaction, that is, it must be transmitted to paper. Not only is it impossible to keep the conversation in memory for the purpose of analysis, but even if it existed in memory, we would have to refer to the taped segment to verify how exactly something was said, requiring hours and hours to find this or that phrase on tape, and the tape (as well as the investigator) would be completely worn out before long. A transcript renders the taped conversation studyable.

However, just as the taped conversation creates an entity different from the interaction itself, so the transcript is yet another artifact. Replacing spoken words with written ones creates a myth of discreteness; utterances that were pronounced imperfectly and in a particular way are rendered as complete words in an idealized form. The most elaborate transcription conventions cannot recreate such features as tone, voice quality, pitch, amplitude, pronunciation, and so on, which constitute any utterance. In a way, I used the transcript not as the object of study but as a representation for the recording; after the repeated listenings that were necessary in order to render the transcript, the lilt of the talk became a permanent recording in my head which I heard each time I referred to the transcript. But this creates a discrepancy between the data as studied and the data presented to the reader. Each reader will necessarily create a text in her/his mind as s/he reads the transcribed segments of talk. Only I and those who have heard the tape will be hearing the same utterances.

Thus there are troubling weaknesses in the use of tape recording and transcript, yet these tools make the analysis possible. Given our understanding of the shortcomings and our awareness of them, we must suspend them and move on to make our analysis.

Accountability in Interpretation

The objection will be raised, But how do you know this is what is really going on? It is just your interpretation. To this I have three replies: (1) the multiplicity of interpretations (2) internal and external evidence and (3) the *aha* factor.

(1) *The multiplicity of interpretations.* I do not offer mine as THE explanation of what is going on. It is simply one explanation, an account of certain aspects of a mass of components in the interaction.

(2) *Internal and external evidence.* Interpretation is not fished out of the air. The fact that something is not provable does not mean that it is not demonstrable. I have followed three procedures to insure that I have not been led astray:

a. There is evidence in the data in the form of recurrent patterns. I do not base interpretation on phenomena that appear once, but rather on phenomena that recur. Therefore, they are demonstrably motivated, not random.

b. There is evidence in the data in the form of participant behavior. For example, misunderstandings or starred sequences are marked by noticeable kinks in interactional rhythm. Or, if I suggest that speaker A is impatient with speaker B, I show evidence in speaker A's behavior (including and especially speech behavior) that indicates impatience.

c. There is accountability in the form of two types of playback. After interpretations are made, they are checked against the independent reactions of participants. Does speaker A report having felt impatient or give other evidence to that effect (e.g. commenting that speaker B was taking a long time getting to the point)? Playback is the litmus test of interpretation.

A further objection may be that, since participants know each other, they have feelings about each other quite apart from the interaction. What if their reactions are not so much to the behavior of the moment as they are to their history of interaction and preconceptions about each other? To correct for this possible bias, a second kind of playback was carried out with objective observers. People who did not take part in the interaction listened to segments of the tape and commented on their reactions and the reasons for them. Thus there is not only accountability but generalizability.

(3) *The aha factor.* My third reply to the doubters of interpretation is perhaps the most significant: If my interpretation is correct, then readers, on hearing my explication, will exclaim within their heads, 'Aha!' Something they have intuitively sensed will have been made explicit. Most discovery, ultimately, is a process of explaining the known. When the subject of analysis is human interaction—a process that we all engage in, all our lives—each reader can measure interpretation against her/his own experience. If an interpretation is misguided, no large number of readers will be deeply impressed by it; it will fade. If it is true, or has grasped a portion of the truth, it will be remembered.

My method then was to record, transcribe, and study the data, to generate hypotheses, and to engage in playback with participants and others to check hypotheses and generate new ones. Transcription of sections used for analysis was checked as well with at least one of the participants.

During the process of transcription I began to get a sense of which episodes I would focus on for analysis. First of all, it bears mention that the most useful unit of study turned out to be the episode, bounded by changes of topic or activity, rather than, for example, the adjacency pair or the speech act. The adjacency pair (for example, question/answer) more often than not, reflected little of what was being done in interaction. The speech act, too (for example, explaining, questioning) was a means by which speakers were trying to achieve some conversational goal. The goal of talk, from the point of view of participants, was to have some effect on other participants (e.g. draw out a new member of the group; tell an amusing story). It was within the episode that I could observe how participants went about pursuing interactive goals and what the effects in fact were. (The psychological reality of interactive goals as opposed to speech acts is noted by Gumperz 1982b.) In general, two kinds of episodes called out for study: those that were striking because they seemed to typify an identifiable kind of interaction, and those that involved apparent dissonance. Just as the starred sentence is for linguists a device by which underlying grammatical rules are uncovered, so episodes in which conversational cooperation breaks down can be seen as starred sequences and used to discover conversational control mechanisms that go unnoticed when conversation proceeds smoothly. In other words, these episodes can be used to uncover the system of rules underlying behavior, i.e. interactional grammar. Such starred sequences are those in which there is a noticeable disruption in rhythm, or participants show signs of annoyance or dissatisfaction with the interaction (i.e. Erickson's [1979] 'uncomfortable moments'). Having isolated such episodes and identified the devices that were misunderstood by a participant, I then looked for other occurrences of the same device in interchanges with the same and other participants.

Playback was a sensitive process. Because this was the way that the other members of the group showed me the interaction from their perspectives, it was important for them to direct the session. I had to be careful to wait for them to make comments and not put ideas in their heads or words in their mouths. Therefore, I gave them control of the tape recorder. They could stop it and comment when they liked, and they could start it again when they felt they were finished commenting. In the event, however, that an episode I had singled out for analysis or another participant had commented upon was not the subject of comment by another participant, I did then call attention to the segment. In those cases I began with the most general questions and only as a last resort made specific mention of what I thought might be going on or what another had observed. The playback sessions were recorded for later reference, and to obviate the need to take notes, which might have hampered the spontaneity of comments.

Playback with David, Chad, and Sally had quite a different character from playback with Steve and Peter. Playback with Steve, and to a large extent with Peter, for the most part confirmed my hypotheses about their intentions. In contrast, playback with Chad, David, and Sally often resembled field work with native speakers of an exotic language. They constantly enlightened me about phenomena that I had found puzzling. This difference highlights a basic aspect of my study.

I speak with a particular style, and I participated in the conversation being analyzed. Moreover, the style I shared to some extent with two other people in the group'dominated' the interaction in a sense. Thus, my analysis emerges, in its focus, as an analysis of that style, and the devices used by the other speakers in the group are contrasted with that. This results from the fact that the slower-paced speakers never had a chance to exercise their own devices in extended interaction with each other, because the faster-paced and expressive style of the high-involvement speakers made it difficult or impossible for them to participate. Furthermore, I have an intuitive grasp of the operation of my own strategies. My understanding of the devices I used, and to a great extent those used by Peter and Steve, was immediate and unequivocal. In contrast, the reactions of the others in the group and the intentions of their devices often had to be explained to me during playback.

This imbalance led to another danger as well. There are times that the analysis may have a ring of self-congratulation, showing that the devices my friends and I use are successful, whereas those used by others in the group cause trouble. I tried to avoid this; I had no conscious intention to imply value judgment. My hypothesis was unequivocally that any devices can be successful when interactants share expectations about their meaning and use, and any devices can cause trouble when such expectations are not shared. However, it is the nature of conversational habits that one's own way of saying things seems self-evidently appropriate, just as the word for chair in one's own language seems to reflect what a chair is, while words for chair in other languages seem like translations. Therefore, this study is necessarily—as a result of the nature of the interaction and my own expertise as a speaker of a particular style—an explication of a high-involvement strategy. I have tried to be diligent in my research on the other strategies involved; I have tried to be fair in my presentation of those findings. Ultimately, however, it will have to remain for speakers of other styles to give a full account of the operation of their own strategies and consequent devices.

The Thanksgiving Conversation

It is time to proceed to the analysis of talk at Thanksgiving dinner, to see what constitutes conversational style and how it works in interaction. In the following chapter the participants are introduced. Nonetheless, readers may need, as they proceed through analysis and quoted segments of conversation, to be reminded of who is who. For this reason, Appendix II provides a brief recap of key information about the participants.

Ideally, a complete transcript of the conversation analyzed should be included as an appendix, but the transcript covers two hundred and fifty pages and would constitute a second volume. Therefore, regrettably, only those segments that I use as examples are presented. I have tried to be liberal in the inclusion of examples, and I am told they succeed in giving the flavor (what Hymes [1974a] calls the key) of the interaction. (Anyone who would like to receive a complete transcript, for the price of duplication, should contact the author.) Because of this omission, however, and by way of introduction to the following chapter introducing participants, I decided to give an overview of the conversation from the point of view of topics discussed. I would like to comment on the results of that effort.

Topic analysis

The dinner conversation included talk on 38 identified topics. I made an initial attempt to count who raised the topics, but I shall not report these findings because the question of who raised a topic turned out to be exceedingly complex, and reporting findings in terms of numbers would be misleading. It is often the case in discourse analysis that, much as a phenomenon may seem discrete in theory, trying to identify instances of that phenomenon in actual interaction yields more equivocal than clear cases, the issues raised by attempts to classify the phenomena turning out to be more enlightening than the classification results. I shall illustrate with examples from segments that will be seen in more detail in the following chapters.

A first glance suggests that the topic of adoption was raised by Peter. After a pause in the conversation, Peter called out from the kitchen, telling about an article he had read that reported the finding that the IQ's of adopted children more closely resemble those of their biological parents than those of their adoptive parents. This was followed by a story round in which other participants told about adopted children they had known. But although Peter clearly 'raised' the topic, the fact that it became a topic for extended talk was the work of the other participants. If no one else had picked up on Peter's comment, would we then say that he had raised a topic? One does not count every comment as a possible new topic but defines as a topic those comments that are picked up and developed by the group. Furthermore, the fact that the conversation developed along the lines of adoption, rather than, for example, IQ's, is also the doing of other speakers than Peter. In fact a later discussion, classified by the topic *social class,* was occasioned by Peter mentioning the same article with a focus on IQ's. Perhaps he intended to raise that topic the first time.

In other cases it is even less clear who raised a topic. Just as a pause can be attributed to one speaker or another, depending on who is perceived as having the floor, so it is open to interpretation who is responsible for the creation of a topic. For example, one speaker may pick up on a comment by another that was not intended to begin a new topic. Furthermore, how much talk needs to be devoted to a topic for it to be counted as such?

Both these ambiguities can be seen in a segment in which Steve called attention to the tape recorder. Chad then asked about my reasons for taping. I explained briefly about my research on conversation, and Chad commented, 'That's like Erving Goffman kind of stuff'. I then exclaimed, 'Oh, you know Erving Goffman?' and Chad and I talked for some time about Goffman's work. I have designated the topic of this segment *Goffman,* and I have considered the beginning of this segment to be Steve's remark about the tape recorder; that and Chad's question about my research were entry talk to that topic. However, it could be interpreted that the topic of talk was my research. Or was it first the tape recorder, then my research, then Goffman? And who raised the topic? Chad was the first to mention Goffman, but if I had not picked up on this (I could have said 'Yes', or 'Not really, what I really do is ...', or 'Never heard of him') and the conversation might have continued as a discussion of my work, or ended. In fact, Steve really brought up the topic by turning attention to the tape recorder in the first place. Finally, all of this begs the larger question of how much it mattered what we were talking about. In some sense, what was really going on was *getting to know each other,* and Chad and I were engaged in what Goffman (hm hm) would call presentation of self.

In other words, caution is recommended in interpreting motivations from taxonomized data. It is always necessary to consider what was done by what was said (as stressed by Labov and Fanshel), and to consider the stream of behavior rather than isolating parts.

A final example is the topic called *New York,* which can be traced to a comment by Chad. Sally had been telling that she was served a bagel with ham on the airplane, and Chad remarked, 'That's what I expected to find in New York was lots of bagels'. Steve then asked Chad some questions about his recent trip to New York, but before long the conversation turned to a discussion of New York geography in which only the three native New Yorkers participated. A determination of who raised the topic of New York would have to credit Chad, but would a reader not then be surprised to find that Chad was very little in evidence in the ensuing conversation? In many people's minds, raising a topic would entail controlling it.

With these cautions in mind, readers may refer to the diagrams in Appendix III that indicate the topics discussed (as I judged and named them), the time spent on them, the people who participated, and how they came up. It is noteworthy that during the two hours and 40 minutes taped there were only a few instances (and these are noted in the diagram) in which talk divided into two parallel conversations. The vast majority of the time the six participants formed a single conversational group.

Because of the complexity of discourse processes, which has been suggested by the discussion of topic, I have refrained from making judgments about participants' intentions to 'dominate,' or 'control' the conversation, an omission that has struck some readers as a weakness. My approach strikes some as a seeking after false harmony. Mine is a rhetoric of good intentions. 'Look', I say, 'these problems arise even when everyone has good intentions'. 'What,' they ask, 'of bad intentions? What of bad will, power struggles, picking a fight?' Such a story can be told, I am sure, but I am not the one to tell it. That bad feelings can arise when one (or more) person is seeking to dominate, to manipulate, to wield power, can come as no surprise. What I wish to demonstrate—and what may come as a surprise—is that bad feelings and imputation of bad motives or bad character can come about when there was no intention to dominate, to wield power, to engender in others the reactions (possibly negative) that were engendered.

CHAPTER 3

The Participants in Thanksgiving Dinner

At 4 P.M. on November 23, 1978, six people gathered for Thanksgiving dinner in Berkeley, California. The guests arrived; they greeted each other, chatted, then sat down to eat turkey, cranberry sauce, and sweet potatoes. The table was set at the beginning and cleared at the end; dishes were washed. Guests left; the host closed the door behind them. And all the while they talked. When the guests returned to their homes and the host retired to the restored quiet of his postdinner house, it was from the talk more than anything else that they gleaned their impressions of the evening and the people who participated in it.

In many ways this dinner in Berkeley was like countless others (some larger, some smaller) that were taking place at the same time, or were ending, or were about to begin. But this was a particular place and time, and these were particular people, gathered at a specific time in their lives, with histories and hopes connecting and separating them. We cannot study every Thanksgiving dinner. We cannot study everything about this one. But we can closely examine the taperecorded conversation of the six people at this dinner and, thereby, glimpse the ways in which their talk worked for them on this occasion.

The dinner, a potluck (in the style that is popular among people of this age living in California at this time) is held at the home of Steve, a 33-year-old musician and music teacher. The first to arrive are Peter and Sally. Peter, 35, is a management analyst at a university. Sally, 29, is a musician. I am the next to arrive. I am 33 and a graduate student at the

University of California, Berkeley. Finally, David and Chad knock at the door, and I let them in. David is 29. He is an artist who also works as a sign language interpreter. Chad will be 30 the next day; he is a writer at a film studio. One more guest will arrive late, after dinner: Victor, 37, an engineer who is deaf.

The guests have come from a range of places. Like Steve, David and I live in Berkeley. Peter has driven from his home elsewhere in the East Bay and has picked Sally up at the airport, where she arrived from her home in Canada. Chad, who lives in Los Angeles, has been visiting David.

Traveling back in time, where did these people grow up? Steve, Peter, and I in New York City; David in Riverside, California and Chad in Los Angeles, California; Sally in London, England. Continuing further back, where did our parents grow up, and their parents, in the process that would lead to this dinner? Steve's and Peter's parents are Jewish and from New York, where their grandparents emigrated from Poland and Russia. My parents, also Jewish, were born in those East European countries and completed their growing up in New York. This backing up of generations uncovers a new overlap: Chad's mother, of Italian descent, was born and raised in New York City; his father is from Los Angeles, of Scotch and English extraction. David's parents, too, are of Irish, Scotch, and English background, but they grew up in North Dakota and Iowa. Sally's father, born and raised in England, was Jewish, and his parents were from Poland—yet another mingling of roots. Her mother is American, from an upper New York State family. Thus the ethnic and geographic strands separate and weave in a braid through the generations.

What bonds bring these people together on this afternoon? Steve is the hub. Peter is his brother. I have been Steve's friend for nearly 20 years, since we met at summer camp when we were 14. Steve and Sally lived together as partners for six years; they have lived apart for four. David has been Steve's good friend for four years. Chad has been David's good friend since college. Victor is David's lover.

And with what feelings and thoughts do they arrive? Steve is the host. He is pleased to have his friends and family in his home. Throughout the evening he will be concerned with making people comfortable and keeping things orderly and attractive. Peter is pleased to be with his brother on Thanksgiving, one of his favorite holidays. He is glad to see Sally and me, both of whom he described as 'like family', though he hasn't seen us much lately. Sally is now a guest in the house where she was once resident, but she notices that she feels quite comfortable. It is rather like coming home for a visit to the house where you grew up: both familiar and foreign. For me, this house is as near to my turf as any that is not mine. I know well and like everyone who will be here, except David's friend Chad, but I have heard about him and I expect to like him. My only apprehension concerns Victor. I have had some uncomfortable moments in encounters with him, and I am hoping they will not be repeated. David is glad to be spending Thanksgiving with Steve and his friends, although he is perhaps a bit concerned about his place in the group: Steve, Sally, Peter, and I seem, in a way, like a unit. David is concerned that his friend Chad like his friends and be liked by them. He knows too that when Victor arrives, he will have to assume the role of interpreter, and this will radically alter his interaction in the group. Chad is looking forward to the dinner, for he has heard about the people involved and he believes he will find them interesting. He is also a bit nervous because he will be the only stranger. Perhaps he is a bit intimidated, because people one has heard much about often seem larger than life.

Each person has professional concerns on her/his mind. Steve is about to perform a major recital; the following week he will be the soloist with a local orchestra. In addition, his students, both adults and children, are having various successes and problems, and he is concerned with their progress. Peter is anticipating a raise in the near future; he is thinking about meetings and decisions that have occupied him at work. Sally has come to the Bay Area to perform a series of recitals. I am about to begin writing my dissertation. This makes me something of a participant/observer in all conversations, including this one, which I will tape. (The decision to base my dissertation on this very conversation has not yet been made.) David will soon be taking a difficult test for certification as a sign interpreter. Chad has recently traveled cross country with a tour sponsored by the production company he works for. The promotional event was Chad's idea, so its realization is a source of satisfaction to him. He is also concerned with a creative writing project he is engaged in.

In addition to their professional lives, all of these people are preoccupied with their private lives. Each one is bound in a network of connections to others not present. Sally, Peter, and Chad are recently separated from partners, and David is about to be so.

The participants' interests and concerns overlap in some ways and diverge in others. There are two musicians (Steve and Sally); a painter (David); two writers (Chad and I); two involved in the world of the university (Peter and I). Three geographical backgrounds are represented, as well as relationships of varying degrees of closeness: siblings (Peter and Steve); former partners (Sally and Steve); as well as friends of varying degrees of intimacy and frequency of contact ranging from Steve and me, friends for nearly 20 years, to new acquaintances (Chad and everyone there except David). There are cases of shared ethnic background; there are two women and four men. Sexual orientation splits the group yet another way: Steve, David, and Chad are gay; Peter, Sally, and I are heterosexual. As the conversation proceeds, these and other alliances appear and recede, either dominating the group discussion or creating parallel discussions.

Each person in the group has a mix of expectations and anxieties about how the others will feel about him or her and how s/he feels about the others. As they engage in conversation, their interests will lead them into group or dyadic discussions in which their foci will temporarily coincide, or just miss each other, or miss each other entirely. Each participant will move to the center of attention at some point, when her/his interests come into focus. Steve and Sally will talk about music; Peter will talk about aikido (he is a brownbelt), and about his children. David will be looked to as the expert on sign language, Sally on cooking, I on language and communication. Chad will be asked about his home and his work. Events in the relationships of some of those present will be discussed. Throughout, everyone will talk about the food.

Everyone expected to have conversation during this gathering, but their notions of what sort of conversation this would be and how it would be effected was necessarily different for different members of the group. The myriad and subtle calibrations of talk that have been discussed and not discussed in the literature created impressions that each person made on the other people, and ultimately the impressions that each had of the dinner gathering as a whole.

In recalling Thanksgiving dinner, Steve said he felt that it had been a terrific evening. The conversation had been lively and satisfying; he had had a great time. This coincided with my impression.

Peter's recollection was slightly less enthusiastic. He said it had been 'successful' but not 'ecstatic'. He recalled that the conversation had been 'competitive', and he remarked that, although he can hold his own in such a conversation, he is not fully comfortable doing so. To explain, he said that he does not live in Berkeley or New York, and most of his friends are not so intellectual as many of Steve's friends.

Sally recalled that it had felt like a 'New York evening'. It was 'pretty frenetic and changeable', she said, and she had been insecure as she always is about her 'place in a rambunctious crowd'. She said that she loves New York style, as long as she gives up trying to be a part of it: 'As soon as I try to keep up, I lose track of myself'. Because she could not participate, there were times when she felt herself verging on boredom. Sally commented that if she had been at a dinner gathering in England, she would have talked more. The conversation would have been 'more consistent'; the whole thing would have been more 'slow moving, logical, and methodical'.

David said that he felt the dinner had been dominated by 'the New York Jewish element'. He remembered the intensity and the pace, and reported that he had felt like an observer, unable to quite 'fit in'. When I pointed out that he had been the center of attention at numerous times, he said, sure, he could be the center of attention or he could be an observer but he could not just 'be part of the flow'. He enjoyed it, he said, but rather as if he had been treated to a show.

Chad recalled that 'the conversation had been all over', but he had enjoyed the dinner very much and gone away happy, feeling that he liked the people he had met: people who talked a lot about things they knew something about. He felt it had been an animated and intellectual discussion.

Participants differed, too, with respect to their recollections of how much they and others had participated. Steve recalled that I had dominated and Peter had talked a lot, too. He felt that Chad had been very quiet, but David had talked rather a lot. Sally identified the 'rambunctious crowd' as being composed of Steve, me, Peter, and David, although she later singled out Steve and me as 'a two-man team'. Peter recalled that Steve had dominated. I had the impression that Steve, Peter, and I had all taken part equally, whereas Sally and Chad had been rather quiet, with David somewhere in between.

In concrete terms, how was talk distributed? Table 1 shows how many contributions and words each participant spoke during the two and a half hours of taped talk.[1]

Counts of contributions and words can be deceptive. For one thing, they do not reflect content or interactional purpose or effect. Second, as

---

[1] I considered a single 'contribution' any uninterrupted flow of talk. If another speaker overlapped and the overlap resulted in the original speaker discontinuing talk which s/he picked up again later, the result was counted as two turns. If an overlap occurred but the original speaker continued without a break in rhythm, it was one turn. In either case the overlap counted as a turn for the second speaker. Nonverbal and contentless utterances, such as 'mhm' or 'wow' were counted as turns when they were uttered against a background of silence in between other speakers' turns. They were not counted as contributions if they were uttered while other speakers continued talking uninterrupted.

Table 1 Number of Conversational Contributions

Name	Conversational turns	Words	Average Words per turn
Deborah	811	8118	10
Steve	594	5223	8.8
Peter	417	4418	10.6
Chad	405	4430	10.9
David	386	3660	9.5
Sally	169	985	5.8

has already been noted, some people strayed out of range of the recorder. I was the only one who remained next to it the entire time; Steve was off in the kitchen quite a lot of the time in the beginning. Nevertheless, some comments made in the kitchen were audible on the tape, if they were directed to people in the adjacent dining area. For most of the period of taping, everyone was within range. There is also the problem of parallel conversations. In some cases, it was impossible to decipher either, but in most cases, at least the outlines of talk were distinguished. Even if it was impossible to tell what someone was saying, at least it was clear from the voice who was saying it. These would appear as contributions but would not be included in word counts, which therefore are not precise but indicative. Table 2 shows words per episode, which indicates relative participation at various times in the interaction.

Thus, some of the impressions left by the conversation on the various participants differed radically from each other, and from the evidence in terms of number of conversational contributions made and words spoken. What was it that made the talk seem 'great' to Steve and me and 'intellectual' to Peter and Chad, while Sally and David experienced it as something definable as 'New York' (and Peter experienced it as 'New York or Berkeley')?[2]

A clue to the style difference that accounted for the discrepancy among impressions of Thanksgiving dinner, came in the form of a comment by David on another occasion during the time when I was beginning my analysis of the data. He had just met my sister, Mimi,

[2]I believe Peter's association of this style with Berkeley represents *his* experience of Berkeley, i.e. visiting Steve and Steve's friends, many of whom are originally from the East Coast.

Table 2 Number of Words Per Episode

	Men, Women	Adoption	Loud Family	Goffman	Life Style	Whorf	LA	Sitting Down	Holidays	Tape Recorder	Wine	Organizations	Food	Bagels	New York	Chad's Job	Cartoons	Quonset Huts	Camp
Peter	198	67	39	88	314	112	0	114	62	0	4	31	374	9	55	174	253	139	77
Deborah	373	126	88	574	204	1317	560	157	164	22	0	69	374	38	140	285	108	203	169
Steve	200	182	32	42	14	13	0	237	93	65	57	0	649	41	191	378	114	269	295
David	107	75	253	23	0	564	0	178	44	66	26	21	197	26	38	69	38	0	35
Chad	117	21	15	350	11	792	990	182	24	11	18	2	35	0	112	524	331	34	16
Sally	15	31	0	6	0	0	0	11	68	0	0	3	51	51	2	57	28	0	0

	School	Social Class	Coffee	Sign Language	Freak Accidents	Finishing Meal	Relationships	Kids & Sex	Learning	Piano Hands	Scolding	Tickets	Post-Dinner	Smoking	Gentleman Pig	Drinks	Words	Words (continued)	Homosexuality	Total
Peter	353	47	15	157	412	20	397	254	128	11	0	21	25	97	0	219	30	8	114	4418
Deborah	214	119	23	432	296	9	297	173	369	110	16	29	30	183	53	357	157	112	168	8118
Steve	57	83	47	221	154	35	67	62	514	180	63	69	164	31	16	250	255	80	3	5223
David	0	0	76	642	64	57	106	22	0	56	0	13	28	31	6	175	305	7	312	3660
Chad	55	1	0	58	147	3	5	0	94	0	6	0	161	106	23	144	14	28	0	4430
Sally	0	7	0	27	9	6	38	0	106	87	7	10	62	4	147	76	1	6	69	985

who was visiting me in California. After he had been talking to her for a while at a gathering at my house, David came up to me with great excitement and animation. 'Your sister talks just like you!' he exclaimed. My interest, of course, could not have been more intense. 'Well, I was talking to her', he said, 'and I told her that I had been in New York last summer. "WHERE"!' David illustrated Mimi's response by tacking on the question 'Where,' very quickly and abruptly, at the end of his question, with falling intonation, like a poke. As he said it, he darted his head in my direction, too, giving the feeling of physically imposing in my conversational space. David repeated, 'Just "WHERE!" Just like that!', as if this were the most peculiar utterance he had ever encountered. 'She didn't say, "Oh, really? Where did you go in New York?" or anything like that. Just "where!" ' Again he imitated the abrupt question and jutted his head toward me. 'And then I realized,' he said, 'that that's what you do. And at first I thought it was really rude, but then I got used to it. And your sister does the same thing. If I hadn't known I would have thought it meant she was bored and wanted the conversation to be over quickly'.

David's comment intrigued me from a number of points of view. That my sister uses a verbal device that I use is not surprising. But David was focusing on a device that both Steve and I use throughout the Thanksgiving conversation. And the fact that David found it so peculiar, that he might in fact find it rude, was a shock to me. How could he think my sister Mimi rude (let alone me)? I was glad that he had gotten used to it, but I knew enough about communication to know that if he found such a device disconcerting, he would continue to do so, and any forgiveness could come only after the fact. David's reaction to my sister's abupt question, and his comment that he found it typical of the sort of thing I do, sent me back to my Thanksgiving tape with renewed focus.[3] Sure enough, I found numerous instances in which devices similar to that were getting Steve, Peter, and me in trouble with Chad, David, and Sally. On the other hand, such devices worked just fine when we used them with each other.

---

[3] I also began to notice this and similar devices in my interactions with other people. For example, at a dinner party I met a fellow New Yorker for the first time. We were talking animatedly to each other. At one point she mentioned her brother, and I asked her, 'What does your brother do?' 'Lawyer', she said, tacking her answer immediately on the tail of my question in a clipped way, with falling intonation. I enjoyed a rush of pleasure at how smoothly our conversation was going, but I thought too of David's observation and realized that this was a way of answering that corresponded to the reduced question form David had noted.

In fact, Steve used precisely the same wording as my sister Mimi in an interchange with Chad. Chad too had recently been to New York, and he made reference to that:

(1)   Chad: 'That's what I expected to find in New York was lòts
          of bágels.

(2)   Steve: Did you fínd them?

(3)   Chad: No, no. What I found were were uh: ... croisuh- crescent rolls?
          and croissant? and all that? ..... thE .. créscent
          rolls mostly. Lots of thát kind of stuff. But it was⌉

(4)   Steve: ⌊Where.

Steve's question (4), 'Where,' comes as an interruption and is spoken with abrupt, falling intonation, just like Mimi's question to David. In fact, the context is almost exactly the same. Steve, too, does not know Chad at this time, and he, too, is asking, 'Where did you go in New York?' Not surprisingly, Chad, when listening to this portion on the tape, like David, said that the question was disconcertingly abrupt and clipped. It made him feel 'on the spot'. That is why his response was hesitant and reserved:

(5)   Chad: Í don't know. ... Í didn't go aroùnd a whole lot for
          breakfast. I was kind of ... stuck in ... the Pláza
          /for a while/ which was interesting.

and his answer trails off at the end.

This is an example of the kinds of conversational devices that will be discussed in the following analysis.[4]

---

[4]For future reference, key information about the participants is recapitulated in chart form in Appendix II. Key to transcription conventions appears at the front.

CHAPTER 4

Linguistic Devices in Conversational Style

After Thanksgiving was over, I had the impression that David's friend Chad had been rather quiet. In addition, I was surprised that there had not been greater rapport between us, since our interests seemed to overlap in a number of ways. Chad, too, in recalling his feelings before the dinner, said that, based on what David had told him about the people he would meet that day, he had been particularly interested in meeting me. This surprised me even more, since I had seen no evidence of such interest. Listening to our conversations on tape confirmed my impression that we never 'really clicked.'

Personal vs. Impersonal Topics

For example, I had tried to draw Chad out by asking him some questions about himself:

. . . .

(1) Deborah: ⌈Yoù live in LÁ?

(2)   Chad: Yeah.

(3) Deborah: ⌈Y'visiting here?

(4)   Chad: Yeah.

(5) Deborah: What do you ⌈dó there?

. . . .

(6)   Chad: uh: I work at Studio Prosuh- ... First Studios. ...

       ⌈a:nd

(7)   Deborah: ⌊Yòu an ártist?

(8)   Chad: No: no.

(9)   Deborah: Writer?

(10)   Chad: Yeah:. I write ... ádvertising copy.

As I listened to this interchange on the tape, I again had the feeling I recalled having had at the time it took place: Chad was being uncommunicative. I was asking him questions to draw him out, and he kept responding with as little information as possible. It seemed as if he did not want to tell me anything. The conversation proceeded this way:

(11)   Deborah: Hmm. I know a lót of people who are writers in LÀ.

(12)   Chad: ⌈Really? Doing what?

                ……

(13)   Deborah: Óne ⌈of them's .. ⌈been writing mòvies and things?

         f

(14)   Chad: ⌊Screenplays. ⌊Everybody's .. scri- ⌊ Really?

(15)   Deborah: They're all trýing to write scr screenplays. [*chuckle*]

(16)   Chad: Yeah. That's what éverybody does in .. LA is wri-

                        Deborah: ⌊Yeah⌋

       try to write scréenplays.

(17)   Deborah: Two of them seem to be doing pretty well.

(18)   Chad: Really? They doing TV, or they doing features, or

       what.

(19)   Deborah: Movies.

       p

(20)   Chad: Really?

(21)   Deborah: Movies.

(22)   Chad: Yeah if they're doing thàt they're doing véry well.

(23)   Deborah: Yeah.

Once the subject turned to the general situation of writers in LA, Chad took an active role in the conversation. He showed interest by volunteering information (16) and evaluations (22) and asking questions (18).

As the conversation proceeded about LA (Chad and I were now

engaged in a dyadic interchange; the others were elsewhere engaged), we achieved a high degree of cooperation. For example, we exhibited a pattern of cooperative sentence-building in which the listener picks up the thread of the speaker and supplies the end of the speaker's sentence, which the speaker then accepts and incorporates into the original sentence without a hitch in rhythm and almost without a hitch in timing.

(1)   Chad: Yeah the town's full of woùld-be wríters, woùld-be

                                  Deborah ⌞I know

           diréctors, woùld-be prodúcers,

(2)   Deborah: ⌞woùld-be áctors,⌝

(3)   Chad: ⌞woùld-be áctors,

(4)   Deborah: Yeah.

(5)   Chad: Yeah it's incrédible.

I pick up Chad's series by offering (2) 'would-be actors' as another in his list, and he repeats this as part of his list (3). Our mutual 'yeahs' (4) & (5) contribute to the sense of harmony and agreement.

    At another point in this segment, it is Chad who reinforces my point.

(1) Deborah: I think everywhere. What's depressing is that when

                           acc

              you think about it, it's probably the same way with

              doctors, and dentists,

(2)   Chad: Dóctors, and déntists, and ... yeah ... and I <u>know</u>

                               [Deborah *chuckles*]

              it's true with lawyers, so

(3) Deborah: Yeah. .. Most people .. Í always figure ... most

                          Chad: ⌞yeah⌟

              people just do their jóbs and get bý ... a:nd ...

              maybe about tèn percent are really gréat, and about

              tèn percent are <u>really</u> <u>horr</u>ible.

(4)   Chad: mhm

                         ...

(5) Deborah: and .. maybe another .... ⌈twenty percent on either end

(6)   Chad: ⌊ /   ?   ./The

              old béll curve comes in agàin.

(7) Deborah: Yeah⌟

In (2), Chad picks up my phrase, 'doctors and dentists', and adds 'lawyers'. When I explain my idea, (3), about people's competence in their jobs, Chad summarizes the significance of what I have just said by calling it 'the old bell curve' (6), and I agree that this is what I had in mind, (7) 'Yeah.'

Thus Chad and I exhibit a flow in our conversation that we both found satisfying. But in listening to the tape I felt that I had shown a lack of interest in Chad by deflecting the conversation from him personally and allowing it to veer off toward jobs in general. There is evidence that I felt just the same at the time because I tried once more to focus on him, with results similar to those that occurred the first time:

(1)　　Chad: So ....

(2)　Deborah: So, but that's a permanent full-time thíng you have?

　　　　　　 So you éat?

(3)　　Chad: Yeah.

(4)　Deborah: That's good.

(5)　　Chad: Uhuh, I just sort of fèll ìnto it. I was kind of

　　　　　　 lúcky, ... and .. I've just been kind of pláying with

　　　　　　 it .. for a while⌉

(6)　Deborah: 　　　　　⌊Did you gó there for that pùrpose?

(7)　　Chad: No. I went there to pay off student loans.

　　　　　　　　　　　......

(8)　Deborah: How'd you get that jób.

(9)　　Chad: My dád's worked there since 1942.

(10)　Deborah: Oh. [*chuckle*] ⌈That helps.

(11)　　Chad: 　　　　　　⌊I didn't get a wríting job but I got

　　　　　　 a job like in the máil room.

Listening to the beginning of this segment of the interchange, I again felt that Chad was being uncooperative. His monosyllabic response, (3) 'Yeah', seemed resistant. Although Chad offered slightly more information in (5), he still seemed reluctant to reveal much, because of his use of hedges ('just sort of', 'kind of', 'just been kind of', 'a while') and internal hesitations. The entire contribution seemed vague and lacking in information. Frustrated by Chad's vagueness, I tried to get him to be more specific by asking (6) 'Did you go there for that purpose?' Again, Chad's response, (7) 'No I went there to pay off student loans', did not seem to me to answer my question. I could not see the connection between paying off loans and choice of a particular city to live in. At this point a two second pause attests to the breakdown in communication. I expected Chad to go on. Because he did not, I asked another question, this time a more direct one: (8) 'How'd you get that job?' Chad's answer to this, (9), was not verbose, but it began to tell something specific. While I was responding with (10) 'Oh that helps', Chad began to talk at length about how he got his job. For the first time I felt that he was participating in the conversation in the way I expected.

During playback with David, I got my first inkling of what might have been going on in these interchanges with Chad. David pointed out that the very reason the conversation became smooth and cooperative when it did, was that the topic had switched from Chad personally to an impersonal topic, LA. He said that he knows Chad is not comfortable talking about himself, especially with someone he does not know very well. Suddenly I saw the irony in my own behavior. Just when Chad was feeling comfortable with the topic, I became uncomfortable, feeling that I had been rude to Chad by switching to a more general topic. Therefore, I refocused the talk on him, with the intention of being nicer to him, but I actually made him uncomfortable, and the conversational rhythm faltered again.

During playback, Chad volunteered the same perspective. He said that he feels on the spot when asked to talk about himself, especially with new acquaintances, and especially about his job. He said that his initial vagueness in the second quoted segment came from that discomfort, but he finally overcame it to answer my direct questions.

Thus I began to see one of the major differences in Chad's and my strategies: expectations about appropriate topics of talk between new acquaintances.

The Enthusiasm Constraint

In order to understand Chad's view of this interchange, it will be useful to back up and look at some earlier interchanges between him and me. Bateson (1972) noted that it is possible to achieve different views of interaction by punctuating the stream of behavior in different places. That is, at the same time that a certain event (X) can be seen as an action causing a reaction (Y), it is simultaneously in itself a reaction to a preceding action (W). And the event (Y) which occurs as a reaction to X will in turn trigger the succeeding event (Z), in a continuous stream. Thus, my conversation with Chad about LA and his job must be seen in light of our preceding interchanges.

Earlier in the Thanksgiving dinner gathering, the conversation had turned to my work. Chad asked what kind of analysis I do on conversation. In response to my explanation, he commented, "That's like Erving Goffman kind of stuff." His comment provoked the following exchange:

(1)   Chad: That's like Erving Góffman kind of stuff.

(2)   Deborah: ⌐Yoú know Erving Góffman?

(3)   Chad: Oh yéah, I lóve his boòks.

(4)   Deborah: Oh, how do you know? I just mét him.

(5)   Chad: Oh díd you?

(6)   Deborah: Yeah.

(7)   Chad: Í always wanted to meet him. I rèad his books ... a

book .. Asýlums. first but that's all
Deborah: ∟Yeah ⌐

because⌐
(8)   Deborah: ⌊I didn't read Asylums but I know it's one of
the brílliant ones.   Chad: ∟But⌐

(9)   Chad: And I just ... ⌐read anóther one.
                                p

(10) Deborah: ∟Did you read Stigma?

(11)   Chad: No. But I've got⌐

(12) Deborah: ∟It's wonderful.

(13)   Chad: I've got ... three or four óther ones

that ⌐are like that.
(14) Deborah: ∟Presentation of Self ⌐in Everyday Life
                                  ∟Presentation of Self in

(15)   Chad: *f*

Everyday Life, ⌐u:m
(16) Deborah: ∟A:nd uh Relations in Public, ... and

Interactional Ritual,

(17)   Chad: Right. Interactional Ritual.

(18) Deborah: I never read thát one.

(19)   Chad: ⌐/Yeàh I've got thát one./

(20)   Peter: ∟What is this?

I recall, when I think about the Thanksgiving conversation, that I felt frustrated at the time because I wanted to hear what Chad thought of

Goffman, and he did not tell me. Yet as I listen to the talk on tape it sounds to me as if I am not giving him a chance to tell me, because I keep cutting him off. My comments (8), (10), (12), (14), and (16) all are timed to overlap with Chad's talk, and they all seem like interruptions, preventing him from saying what he began. How could my conversational device (interruption) so obstruct my purpose (find out what Chad thinks about Goffman's work)?

When I listened to other parts of the tape, in which I talk to Steve and Peter, I got an insight into what may be going on. I was trying to encourage Chad to tell me, not by waiting for him to talk, but by showing him my own excitement and exuberance. The message is in the very pace that I am creating: 'See how excited and interested I am? I can hardly contain myself'. I expect Chad to become equally excited and shout me down. What throws this conversation off is that each time I overlap with Chad he stops what he is saying. That is why I end up looking (and feeling) like a bulldozer. From my point of view, Chad reacts like a basketball player who purposely hurls himself to the floor when an opponent touches him, so that the referee will think he has been pushed hard. By contrast, in conversations with Steve, I become excited and overlap and shout, and Steve matches my volume and shouts right over me—some of the time. Other times he stops and I continue. The overall effect is a balanced interchange. (Examples of this will be presented later.)

The overlap-as-enthusiasm strategy is reminiscent of the *enthusiasm constraint* I discovered for Greek speakers (Tannen 1981a). It is reminiscent as well of a behavioral pattern I have seen on numerous occasions in Greece. When two men become involved in an argument in a public situation, they often shout loudly at each other, and it is very common for one of the two to raise his hand to attack the other physically. Invariably, however, before he can bring his arm forward into his enemy's face, someone—any other man in the vicinity—will grab his outstretched arm and restrain him. It is the knowledge that someone will restrain him that makes it possible for the man to take a swing, and the backward swing of his arm is the complete message to his enemy, 'I am angry enough to hit you.' I suspect that if no one stopped him, and he succeeded in punching the other man, the attacker would be as surprised and mortified as the victim. The message is in the swing, not the attack. Analogously, my message in conversation is the excitement and exuberance that urges me to talk loud and fast with my interlocutor. It is not my intention to hog the floor. I fully expect that others will talk over me.

Although Chad does not participate in this way when I talk to him about Goffman, his verbal devices come closer to such a strategy when we operate as a duet (Falk 1979) in talk with a third party. This happens when Paul asks what we are talking about:

(19) Chad: ⌐ /Yeah I've got thát one./⌉
(20) Peter: ⌐ What is this?   ⌡ What is he? What is he?

(21) Deborah: He's a sociologist, ⌐ who's <u>so brill</u>iant. You have to →
(22) Chad: ⌐ He's just incrédible. He's just →

   Deborah: ⌐ / ?   ?   / →
   Chad: ⌐ incredible. He's <u>witty</u>.

(23) Deborah: a pleasure reading. ⌐ Yeah. You guys háve
(24) Peter: ⌐ which one?   ⌐ Asylums?

(25) Chad: All of 'em.

(26) Deborah: Read Asylums,

(27) Chad: Yeah, that's a <u>good</u> one to read.

(28) Deborah: And the other one I- well read Stigma.
              Chad: ⌐Yeah⌐ ⌐mm⌐

(29) Peter: The what?

(30) Deborah: Stigma.

(31) Chad: Stigma?

(32) Deborah: Well maybe read Presentation of Self

   first. ⌐ /???/
(33) Chad: ⌐ And he does real strange things yknow he goes

   to he talks about gámblers and all this kind of stuff

   and makes all these análogies ... and it's really /?/

In this segment, Chad times his contributions to begin before I have done talking (22, 27, 33); we make similar comments simultaneously (21, 22); he ratifies my comments (26, 27); and he echoes my words (30, 31). He also volunteers information and opinions (33).

In playback, Chad noted that when I questioned him about Goffman, he was intimidated. For one thing, he felt I was the expert and he the novice. Therefore, anything he might say would reveal his relative ignorance, so he preferred that I keep talking, operating on a defensive strategy. I, however, was operating on a camaraderie strategy. Starting from the assumption that we were equals, I tried to establish rapport by throwing out everything I could think of associated with the topic: for example, listing the names of Goffman's books. In typical complementary schismogenetic fashion, this had the effect of overwhelming Chad and intimidating him even more. He commented during playback, 'See how well you know Goffman, how you're rattling off the names of all his books?' The fact that I had not read many of them did not come through; it was overshadowed by the impact of the list. However, in talk aimed at Peter, who did not know anything about the subject, Chad said he felt free to show off what he knew. This highlights the fact that whereas a speaker may not employ a certain strategy in one situation, s/he might well employ it in a different context. Preference for one strategy or another is not absolute, but context-sensitive.

In the discussion with Chad about Goffman, I do the same thing that I do in our later talk about LA: I get a sense that I am doing too much of the talking, so I try to turn the conversation back to Chad. The result is just the same as it is in the other discussion: Chad's strategy becomes more defensive.

(1) Deborah: But ányway. ... How do you happen to know his stuff?
               f - - - - - - -]

(2)   Chad: Cause I reád it.

(3)   Peter: ⌐What do you do?⌐
(4) Deborah: ⌐/ ? ?   ⌐are you in ... sociology or anything?

(5)   Chad: Yeah I read a líttle bit of it. [pronounced *reed*]

(6) Deborah: Hm?

(7)   Chad: I read a líttle bit of it. [pronounced *red*]

(8) Deborah: I mean were you ... uh studying sociology?

(9)   Chad: No.

(10) Deborah: You just heard about it, huh?

(11)   Chad: Yeah. No. I heard about it from a fríend who was a
               sociologist, and he said read this book, it's a good
               Deborah: ⌐uhuh⌐
               book and I read that book 'n⌐
               Deborah ⌐uhuh⌐   Peter ⌐huh

(12) Deborah: I had never heard about him before I started studying
               linguìstics.

(13)   Chad: Really?

(14) Deborah: Yeah.

In answer to my high-pitched question (1) 'How do you happen to know his stuff?' Chad says (2) 'Cause I read it'. This seemed (and seems) to me to be begging the question. Chad seemed to be resisting the obvious question of how he happened to read it. Further, he spoke with a tone that suggests slight annoyance, as if to say, 'I read it, of course. How else?' Peter reacted as I did, because he asked (3) 'What do you do?' at the same time that I asked (4) 'Are you in sociology?' (During playback Peter attested that this was indeed his reaction.) That is, both Peter and I expected Chad to tell how his life—and most likely his work or education—led him to Goffman's books. My question (4) represents my characteristic tactic of asking with a more direct question, when I do not get the information I expect. Again Chad's answer (7) 'I read a little bit of it,' does not explain how he came to read it. Predictably, I follow up by narrowing the focus of my question, giving him a choice: (8) 'I mean were you ... uh studying sociology?' Again, Chad's answer declines to give more than the information immediately requested: (9) 'No.'

At this point I apparently give up trying to elicit information from Chad. However, the matter does not feel closed to me, so I supply a plausible explanation of my own: (10) 'You just heard about it, huh?' Here I seem to be coming to terms with the fact that Chad is not going to furnish the sort of answer I expect, so I settle for my own reconstruction of his unstated answer. At just this point, Chad comes through with what I expected four conversational turns earlier: (11) 'I heard about it from a friend who was a sociologist.' Again, Chad was reluctant to offer information in a field in which he felt I was more competent. Chad noted, during playback, another possible factor in his reluctance to offer information about the source of his familiarity with Goffman's work. The friend who was a sociologist was someone Chad had lived with for many years. Hence, it was an association with personal matters that he did not want to talk about.

This conversation about Goffman preceded the one about LA and Chad's work. The two interchanges exhibit roughly the same pattern (what Pittenger et al. call 'recurrence'). Throughout these conversations, I had the feeling that Chad was withholding and resisting, and I had no idea why. I kept trying to rectify the situation by talking faster, asking him more questions, being more enthusiastic, saying more, and focusing more attention on him personally. It now seems likely that all these devices had the effect of further inhibiting him.

There are at least two major stylistic differences operating here: notions of content (what it is appropriate to talk about) and conversational signals (how it is appropriate to talk about it). The idea that it is appropriate to talk about personal matters with new acquaintances, that people like to talk about themselves, seems like a given to some speakers (e.g. me), whereas for others it is equally obviously not true. Note, of course, that the setting determines appropriateness judgments. Chad may well like to talk about himself with a close friend, if not with someone he has just met.

The Machine-Gun Question

To me, the way in which I asked questions of Chad, with high pitch, rapid rate, fast pacing with respect to preceding comments, and reduced syntactic forms, all signal familiarity and casualness, hence, rapport; that is, such questions are designed to make the other feel comfortable. However, my questions made Chad feel on the spot, rather like my sister's question to David ('Where.') discussed previously. Questions of this sort operate effectively in other segments of the Thanksgiving conversation, specifically, in interchanges among Steve, Peter, and me.

For example, note the following segment. At this point, Peter has commented that his son's teacher believes that television has limited children's fantasy lives, and Steve concurs. I then ask Steve and Peter a series of questions, fast and at times high-pitched, just like those that I earlier asked Chad:

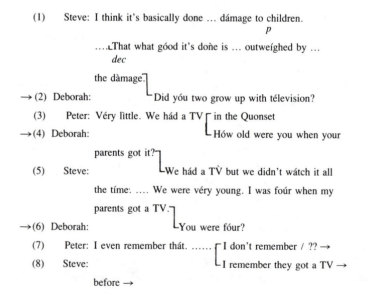

Peter: ?   /⌐
Steve: we moved out of ⌐ the Quónset huts. In níneteen fifty
        foùr.⌐
(9)   Peter: ⌐I remember we got it in the Quonset huts.
→(10) Deborah: [*chuckles*] ⌐You lived in Quónset huts? ..... ⌐When you
        were hów old?

                        .....

(11)   Steve: Y'know my fàther's dentist said to him whát's a Quónset
        hut. ... And he said Gód, yóu must be younger than my
        chíldren. .... He wás. .... Yoùnger than bóth of us.
                        [Sally *sighs*]

The pace of this entire segment is fast, with much overlap and little
pause between utterances. My questions may set the pace, but the
responses are equally fast paced. Peter and Steve overlap with each
other (7, 8) and latch utterances onto preceding ones with no perceptible
pause (5, 9). (The term "latch" is taken from Schenkein 1978.) My
question (2) is latched onto Steve's rather slow-paced observation about
television, (1). My next question, (4), is timed to overlap with Peter's
answer to (2). (Since Peter and Steve are brothers, they are equally able
to answer.) My questions in (10) are high pitched and fast: 'You lived in
Quonset huts?' is a response question, showing my surprise, and 'When
you were how old?' asks for more information in just the same tone.

My question (2), 'Did you two grow up with television?', represents
a shift in focus of the conversation, putting Peter and Steve on the spot
in a personal way, whereas they were previously talking about television in general. They both quickly take up this new tack, and in their
responses they interrupt and repeat each other to answer in tandem. By
the time I ask (4) 'How old were you when your parents got it?' Steve
has just begun to answer my question (2) with his comment (5): 'We
had a TV but we didn't watch it all the time.' He goes ahead with this
comment and then continues to answer my second question by saying,
'I was four when my parents got a TV'. It is interesting to see how the
constructions of the two sentences reflect the shift in focus of Steve's
statements. His first sentence in (5), 'We had a TV but,' echoes Peter's
'We had a TV' in (3). Steve's second sentence in (5) picks up the phrase
'when my parents got a TV' from my question (4), 'How old were you
when your parents got a TV'.

There are two intricate patterns of synchronization here. The first is
Peter's and Steve's 'duetting' (Falk 1979), as they both talk about their

childhood recollections; that is, they jointly hold one side of the conversation. I, meanwhile, am timing my questions to come either as interruptions or at the precise end of Peter's and Steve's sentences—extremely rapid fire. If my rapid questions come at a time when Steve is not prepared to stop talking, he either answers when he is ready or ignores the question completely, depending on how much more he has to say. The first phenomenon has been seen in (5). The second can be seen when Steve ignores my question (10), 'You lived in Quonset huts? ... When you were how old?' Instead of answering, he tells a little story, (11), which he has thought of in connection with Quonset huts.

Note too the compressed nature of question (10), 'When you were how old?' as opposed to the standard form, 'How old were you when you lived there?' The full form would have taken longer to utter, and would have signaled its interrogative intent syntactically. The question as uttered is a reduced form; it is shorter, and its interrogative intent is signaled most saliently by sharp rising intonation. The result of this reduction, combined with the accelerated pace of utterance, is that the question relays the conversational ball faster than would normally be expected, just like the reduced question, 'Where', which was discussed earlier. The effect is intended as a rapport device, by which the metamessage is, 'We are such good communicators, we don't need full forms'. However, when used with someone who does not share this system, the interpretation made by the hearer might be (like David's reaction to the reduced question 'Where'), 'Let's get this conversation over with because you're such a bore'.

In addition, the fast pace, reduced syntactic form, and high pitch of this question are intended to connote casualness, to signal the message, 'Answer this if you like, but if you have something else to say, go ahead, because this really isn't all that important.'' This message gets through; Steve takes the option of not answering the question. It is not the case that the question overlaps with something he has already begun to say, as in (5), where his statement begins immediately after my question (4). Rather, there is a long pause of 1.5 seconds after my question (10), before Steve begins his story (11). As I listen to the tape, I do not mind in the least that he has chosen to tell this story rather than answer my question. I am pleased that he realizes that I would like to hear what he most feels like telling, and that he does not feel he must answer every question I happen to ask. His lack of compulsion about answering my questions frees me to toss them out as exuberantly as I like.

At other times, Steve permits my interruption to change the course of his talk. For example, later in the same episode, he comments that people living in the Quonset huts had rats, and he continues:

(1) Steve: Cause they were built near the swámp. .... We used to
go ... hunting frógs ⌐in the swámps,
(2) Deborah: └Whére wàs it. Whére were yoùrs?
                             f   *acc*

(3) Steve: In the Brónx.
(4) Peter: └ In the Brónx. In the Eást Brònx?
(5) Deborah: How long did you líve in it?⌉
(6) Steve: └Near the swamps? .... Now
there's a big cooperative building.
(7) Peter: └Three years.
(8) Deborah: <u>Three years?</u>
        [*breathy tone*]

In this segment, Steve permits my overlap to become an interruption. When I ask (2), 'Where was it. Where were yours?', he halts his recollection about hunting frogs in the swamps (1) to answer my question in (3). However, when my next question (5) comes, 'How long did you live in it?', he is still answering my previous question with (6) 'Near the swamps? .... Now there's a big cooperative building.' In other words, he has taken one question (2) and allowed it to determine his next contributions, but he ignores another, (5), because it is too soon after his answer to (2). My question (5) is actually answered by Peter, who is not otherwise engaged (and who throughout the evening is attentive to my questions and needs, as I am to his).

When Steve listened to this conversation on the tape, he affirmed that it was a fine conversation. He was not troubled by my rapid questions; he felt they showed interest, and he found their pace appropriate to the dynamic nature of the talk. It was just this dynamic quality, he averred, that made the conversation satisfying. Peter did not find the pace unusual either, but he noted that he was having some trouble staying in there.

There are many other segments of the Thanksgiving dinner conversation that show that Steve and I use rapid questions in the same way. In one, Chad is again the unfortunate target. The beginning of this segment has already been reported and discussed (p. 53). It is the discussion in which Chad mentions his trip to New York, and Steve asks him where he went there. Following is the extended segment.

(1)　Chad:　'Thát's what I expected to find in New York was lòts of
　　　　　　　　acc

　　　　　　bágels.

(2)　David:　Yeah lots of bágels and when you go to Bóston you

　　　　　　expect to find ⌈beáns.

(3)　Steve:　　　　　　　　　⌊Did you fínd them?

(4)　Chad:　No, no. What I found were were uh: ... croisuh-

　　　　　　crescent rolls? and croissant? and all that? .....

　　　　　　thE .. créscent rolls mostly. Lots of thát kind of

　　　　　　stuff. But it was⌉

(5)　Steve:　　　　　　　　⌊Where.

(6)　David:　Croissant.

(7)　Chad:　Í don't know. ... Í didn't go aroùnd a whole lot for

　　　　　　breakfast. I was kind of ... stuck in ... the Pláza /for
　　　　　　　　　　　　　　　　　　　　　　　　　　　　　pp

　　　　　　a while/ which was interesting.

(8)　Deborah:　Yòu stayed at the Pláza?

(9)　Chad:　Yeah.

(10)　Deborah:　⌈Hooooooooo!⌉

(11)　Steve:　　　　　　⌊Were yóu on the ⌈Wést Side at all?
　　　　　　　　acc

Steve responds to Chad's comment (1) that he expected to find
bagels in New York by asking (3) 'Did you find them?' In this he cuts
off the end of David's humorous observation, (2). Chad's reply, (4), to
Steve's question is fairly long but repetitive, slowed down by a filler
(uh:), a false start ('croisuh-'), repetition and rewording ('crescent
rolls', 'croissant,' 'crescent rolls'), what I call 'buffer language' ('and
all that?', 'that kind of stuff'), and pauses. Steve interrupts this reply to
ask (5) 'Where.' The contrast between Chad's diffuse and repetitive (4)
and Steve's abrupt question (5) could not be more dramatic. In (7) Chad
replies to Steve's question with another diffuse contribution. (7) begins
with a hedge ('I don't know'), proceeds to a pause, has more hedges ('a
whole lot,' 'kind of') and has more pauses before reaching the substan-
tive answer that he ate breakfast at the Plaza Hotel, after which his voice
trails off. It has already been postulated, as confirmed by Chad, that the
abruptness of Steve's question probably took him aback and, therefore,
slowed him down even more than ordinarily might have been his style.

No sooner does Chad get this information out, than I ask a question which is really a back channel response (Yngve 1970), encouraging him to continue (8) 'You stayed at the Plaza?' In this instance, as has been seen elsewhere, rephrasing Chad's statement as a question is meant to show great interest: his words have made an impression. Chad's muted and characteristic response, (9) 'Yeah', is met with yet another exclamation from me, this time a high-pitched nonverbal one: (10) 'Hooooooooo!' At this point, Steve jumps in with (11) 'Were you on the West Side at all?' His question is spoken quickly, with high pitch, ends with marked rising intonation, and is latched onto the preceding utterance.

In another segment of conversation, it is clear that Peter too uses the strategy of quick questions to show interest. In the second hour of taped conversation, David is talking to the group about sign language. He has just explained the three signs he knows for the word *Christmas* and told what they symbolize.

(1) David: So: and thís is the one that's Bèrkeley. This is

the Bèrkeley ... sign for .. for ┌ Christmas.
                                  │ p
(2) Deborah: └ Do yòu figure óut
                                       f

those .. those um correspòndences? or do- when you
                   David:'-/?/ ┘

learn the signs, /does/ somebody télls you.

(3) David: Oh you mean ┌ watching it? like
(4) Deborah: └ Cause I can imagine knówing that sìgn, ...

and not .. figuring out that it had anything to do with

the decorátions.

                    ...

(5) David: No. Y you knów that it has to do with the

decorátions.┐
(6) Deborah: └ Cause somebody télls you? Or you figure it óut.
                          David:└ No ┘

(7) David: Oh. ... You talking about mé, or a deàf person. │
(8) Deborah: └ Yeah. ┘   │ You. You.

(9) David: Me? uh: Someone télls me, ùsually. ... But a lót of

em I can tèll. I mean they're óbvious. .... The bétter

I get the mòre I can tell. The lónger I do it the mòre

I can tell what they're talking about.

.....Withóut knowing what the sign is.⌐

(10) Deborah: huh. ⌐ That's interesting. ⌐

(11) Peter: ⌐ But how do you

leaŕn a new sígn?

....

(12) David: How do I leaŕn a new sígn?⌐

(13) Peter: ⌐Yeah. I mean supposing...

Víctor's talking and all of a sudden he uses

a sign for Thanksgíving, and you've never séen it

before.

My questions (2), (4), and (6) and Peter's questions (11) and (13) are timed to overlap or latch immediately onto David's preceding comments. In contrast, David's comments follow our questions after normal or even noticeable (5, 12) pauses.

My question (2) about whether David figures out the sign symbolism for himself or is told about it, not only is latched onto David's fading comment (1), but is spoken loudly, and whereas David was making a general statement about sign, I am suddenly turning the focus on him personally, as I do in previous examples with Chad and Steve. I later learned (from David's comments during playback) that abrupt questions catch him off guard. That is why he is taken aback at this point and hesitates by rephrasing the question. I then interrupt David's rephrasing to give more information to illustrate my question (4). The fact that David hesitated indicated to me that I had not given him enough information; however, the real trouble was not that, but the suddenness of my question and the fact that it shifted from a general to a personal topic without outward warning. What David really wanted was a slower paced conversation.

David answers my question (4) by commenting (5) on my illustration, but he does not answer my initial question (2) of HOW he knows that the sign symbolizes a certain thing (the Christmas sign symbolizing decorations was an example). I, therefore, use my now-familiar strategy of asking again, becoming more specific. My question (6) 'Cause somebody tells you? Or you figure it out', is latched onto David's comment (5) 'You know that it has to do with the decorations'. Once more David stalls by asking (7) for clarification of the question. Again, his question comes after a filler, a pause, a slight stutter at the beginning of his sentence: 'Oh. ... You you talking about me, . . .'. Again, I clarify in machine-gun fashion: (8) 'Yeah. You. You'. David then answers my question to my satisfaction and is rewarded with an appreciative (10) 'huh' and a comment 'That's interesting', which overlap with his answer.

The rhythm of this interchange is significant. As with Chad in the LA discussion presented earlier, the rhythm is a pattern of answer-question, pause, answer-question, pause. Normally, a question and answer are seen as an 'adjacency pair' (Sacks, Schegloff, and Jefferson 1974), and in a smooth conversation, they are rhythmically paired as well. The differences in David's style on the one hand, and Peter's and mine on the other, however, create pauses not between an answer and the following question, but between our rapid questions and his delayed answers. Each resultant rhythmic pair, then, is made of David's answer and the next adjacent question. This is typical of the way in which stylistic differences create obstructions in conversational rhythm. The jerky rhythm is created by the difference in expectations about how much time should appropriately lapse between utterances in the conversation. (It has been seen that Chad is perfectly capable of overlapping and interrupting in other conversations, and Steve, Peter, and I allow long pauses during other sorts of talk, for example, during a serious discussion of emotional problems.)

A variety of linguistic features make these questions seem like machine-gun fire, including high pitch, reduced syntactic form, fast rate of speech, and directness of content. In addition, the effect of all these features is intensified by the pace with which the question is fired in conversation, that is, the time that is permitted to elapse before the question is posed. In this, the quick question is one aspect of fast pacing that is one of the most salient characteristics of the high-involvement strategy under analysis.

Overlap and Pace

In the excerpt previously presented (p. 68) about New York, Steve and I were so quick with our responses, so animated in our interest in New York as a topic of talk, that Chad got lost in short order. Steve's question (11), 'Were you on the West Side at all?', did not spark a discussion with Chad about his visit to New York. Rather, it launched

Steve and me, and to some extent Peter, on a discussion of our own
about New York. We fired and answered questions and overlapped in
the continuing discussion.

In answering Steve's question about whether he went to the West
Side, Chad mentions a restaurant he went to downtown. Steve then
corrects, 'No, I mean the <u>Upper</u> West Side'. Chad says he doesn't
know, so I hypothesize for him that he did not go there, and I ask a
question to verify this. The question (1), however, elicits a terse response from Chad. The one it engages in conversation is Steve:

(1) Deborah: Próbly not. Dju go to the Coliséum?
                              acc

(2)   Chad: No.

(3) Deborah: Probly he didn't go to the West Side⌐
                   acc, p

(4)   Steve: ⌐Cóliséum?!
                                                 f

(5) Deborah: Thàt's where the beginning of the West 'Síde is.
                   acc

(6)   Steve: Oh right.

(7)   Peter: ⌐Wwhàt's the Coliséum.
      Steve: ⌐/?/

(8) Deborah: Fifty ninth and uh:

(9)   Chad: [*sings*] Ea:st Si:de, We:st Si:de.

(10) Peter: What ís it.

(11) Deborah: What ís it? It's a big exposítion center.

(12) Steve: And office building.
      David: ⌐/?/
(13) Peter: ⌐By fifty ninth. And Columbus Circle.

(14) Deborah: ⌐mmm⌐

               ....

(15) Steve: Rremember where ⌐W I N S used to be?

(16) Deborah: No.⌐

(17) Steve: ⌐Then they built a big huge skyscraper there?

(18) Deborah: No. Whère was thát.

(19) Steve: Right where Central Park West met Broádway. That
                   acc

(20)　　Peter:　⌐building shaped like that. [*Makes a pyramid with hands*]
　　　　　　　└Did ⌐I give you too much? [*re turkey*]
(21)　Deborah:　　　　└By Columbus Círcuit? ... that Columbus Círcle?
(22)　　Steve:　　　　　　　　　　　　└Right on Columbus Círcle.

　　　　　　　Hére's Columbus Circle, ... ⌐here's Central Park West,
(23)　Deborah:　　　　　　　　　　　　└Nòw it's

　　　　　　　the Huntington Hártford Museum.
(24)　　Peter:　└Thàt's the Huntington Hártford, right?

(25)　　Steve: Nuhnuhno. ... Hére's Central Park West, hére's
　　　　　　　　　　　　　　　　　　　Deborah: └Yeah.

　　　　　　　Broadway. We're going nórth, thìs way? ... and
　　　　　　　　　　　　　　　　　　　Deborah: └ uhuh ⌐
　　　　　　　here's thís building hère. The Huntington Hártford is
　　　　　　　is ⌐on the Soúth side.
(26)　Deborah:　　└on the óther- across. Yeah, rightrightrightright

　　　　　　　⌐And nów that's a new building with uh¬
(27)　　Steve: └And there was ...　　└ and⌐　　　│there was a-
　　　　　　　stóres here, and the upper second floor was W I N Ś.
　　　　　　　　　　　　　　　　　　Deborah:└ oh: ⌐
　　　　　　　... And we listened to:

(28)　Deborah: Now it's a round place with a: movie theatre.

(29)　　Steve: Now- there's a roun- No. The next .. néxt block is but
　　　　　　　... but ... <u>this</u> is a huge skýscraper right there.
　　　　　Deborah: └ oh ⌐　　　　　　　　　　　　└ oh, yeah.

　　　　　　　　　　　　　　......

(30)　Deborah: hm¬
(31)　　Steve:　└It's amazing.
(32)　Deborah: I never <u>knew</u> where W I N Ś was.
(33)　　Steve: That was my <u>haunt</u> cause I went down for children's concerts.

Beginning with Steve's question to Chad about whether he went to the West Side in New York, Steve and I launch an intense discussion of the geography of Columbus Circle. We were joined occasionally by Peter, but Peter noted during playback that he does not know New York City as well as Steve does, because he never lived in Manhattan as an adult. Therefore, he felt somewhat intimidated during this discussion. The pace of this conversation is extremely rapid, and includes complex subtopics within the overall topic of Columbus Circle. For example, Steve asks

> (15) Rremember where ⌐W I N S used to be?

WINS is a New York radio station that was popular when we were young. I answer (16) 'No', but Steve proceeds with (17) very quickly, as if I had not answered this way at all.

> (17) Then they built a big huge skyscraper there?

I repeat my negative reply (18) 'No', and ask 'Where was that?'

As Steve explains to me where W I N S was, there is rapid and loud overlap as Steve, Peter, and I all repeat each other's phrases to show agreement. I suggest (21) 'By Columbus Circle?' (which is not a real question, since its location at Columbus Circle is the reason Steve brought W I N S up in the first place). Steve repeats this phrase (22) 'Right on Columbus Circle', timing his agreement to overlap with my utterance. He has had a clue in the form of my false start (21) 'Columbus Circuit' and, therefore, need not wait for me to complete the correct phrase. Steve then continues his explanation, with hardly a hitch in timing:

> (22)   Steve: Right on Columbus Circle. Hére's Columbus Circle, ...
>
>   hére's Central Park West,

I then interrupt his explanation (22) to show that I understand well enough to supply a new landmark of my own:

> (23) Deborah: Nów it's the Huntington Hártford Museum.
>
> (24)   Peter: ⌐Thàt's the Huntington Hártford, right?

It is particularly interesting to note Peter's contribution (24). Peter is able to use his familiarity with the rhythmic patterns of our talk to participate, even though he is not familiar with the material under discussion. Peter suggests 'That's the Huntington Hartford, right?' as if he had reason to believe that this is correct. In fact, he is echoing, or piggy-backing, my erroneous comment (23). It is highly unlikely, were he to mistake Steve's geography lesson independently, that he would make precisely the same mistake that I did. It seems clear, therefore, that he picks up my comment (23) and uses it as the basis for his own (24), waiting just long enough after I began talking for him to know what I would say. He took a calculated risk, assuming that I would be right. Although I was wrong and, hence, he was wrong, he did succeed in participating smoothly in the interchange. This is a testament to the fact that sharing conversational style in the form of pacing and overlap habits is sufficient for participation; specific knowledge of the topic is less so.

Because the building Steve has in mind is not the Huntington Hartford Museum, Steve tells us that we are wrong. He says, (25) 'Nuhnuhno,' backing up to repeat his explanation in precisely the same intonation that he began in (22):

(25)   Steve: Nuhnuhno. ... Hére's Central Park West, hére's

Broadway.

I am now even more anxious to show that I understand, because I have been wrong once, so I complete Steve's sentence with him:

(25)   Steve: The Huntington Hartford is is ⌐ on the South side.
(26) Deborah: ⌊ on the other- across.

Yeah, rightrightrightrightright.

My quintuplet machine-gun 'rights,' (26), correspond to Steve's triple machine-gun 'no's', (25); I need a few more to counteract my previous error in (23).

This segment demonstrates as well how our rapport strategy, urging us to reach agreement, throws us into exaggerated forms of our habitual style when it is threatened. Because I do not really understand which building Steve has in mind, I am even more eager with my overlaps and offers to finish his sentences about where it is. The rapid-fire 'no's' and 'rights' are a symptom of this too.

The next way that I try to rectify my error and show understanding is to offer my idea of what is there now:

(26) Deborah: ..... ⌜And nów that's a new building with uh:⌝
(27)   Steve: ⌞And there was   ...⌞ and⌟   ⌞there was

          a- stóres here, and on the upper second floor was W I N Ś.

          ... And we listened to:

At this point Steve is following up what he started in (15), that is, the location of the radio station. Because he chooses to override my overlap (26) with his explanation (27), I repeat it:

(28) Deborah: Now it's a round place with a: movie theater.

The next line of conversation is a most intriguing form of evidence for the drive to repeat to show agreement.

(29)   Steve: Now- there's a roun- No. The next .. néxt block is

          but ... but ... <u>this</u> is a huge skýscraper right there.
      Deborah: ⌞oh⌟   ⌞oh, yeah.

In (29) Steve begins automatically to repeat my phrase 'now it's a round building with a movie theater', to ratify my offer of understanding. But in fact he cannot do so, because I have been wrong again (in fact, I have no idea at all where WINS used to be), so he must stop himself from agreeing, to correct me again. The false start is a testament to the strength of his impulse to repeat an interlocutor's phrase that has been offered as a show of rapport, that is, to incorporate the other's offer into his own statement. It is interesting to note, too, that Steve's correction, (29) 'this is a huge skyscraper', is a repetition of his earlier statement, (17) 'Then they built a big huge skyscraper there?' 'Huge skyscraper' seems to be operating as a formulaic phrase; and after all this heated negotiation, Steve is right back where he began in his description.

Now Steve and I have finally agreed upon the site for the building that Steve is talking about, or at least he has disabused me of my specific confusion of it with another building. There is then a slight pause, in which I say (30) 'Hmm' and Steve says (31) 'It's amazing', both of which seem to be meant to fill the quiet after the storm. Then, in (32), I explain why I have been so inept in placing the building Steve has tried to recall:

(32) Deborah: I never <u>knew</u> where W I N S was.

In (33) Steve justifies his greater expertise and perhaps also his intense preoccupation with getting the geography of the area right:

(33)   Steve: That was my <u>haunt</u> cause I went down for children's

concerts.

Sally's reaction, when listening to this interchange on the tape, was to laugh. She noticed, first of all, how the topic of New York got taken away from Chad. Then she commented on the intensity of the discussion in which Steve and I became embroiled. 'I find it incredibly funny', Sally said. 'I love it. It's ultimate New York'. What she found funny was that Steve was so intent on establishing just which street and which building he was thinking of, and that I shared that earnestness. Sally remarked that while she loves listening to such discussions, she could never participate in one because she could not distinguish between what is important and what is not. 'I would never talk so intensely about something so insignificant', she said. It seems to her that in New York conversation, anything is important, just by virtue of being talked about. To her, the Coliseum discussion is a great sound and fury signifying nothing.

The fact that Sally felt she could not distinguish between what is important and what is not is strong evidence that different signaling systems are at work. In contrast to Sally's reaction to this discussion as remarkable, when Steve listened to it on tape, he had no particular reaction, except to smile and note that it had been an enjoyable evening. To him (as to me), it was just a good conversation.

Thus, rapid rate of speech, overlap, and latching of utterances are devices by which some speakers show solidarity, enthusiasm, and interest in others' talk. The resulting fast pace greases the conversational wheels when speakers share expectations about use of these devices.

It is probably not a coincidence that this interchange, which seems typical of New York style in its intensity, pace, overlap, loudness, and emphasis on rapport, was about New York. It seems to be the case that a conversation about a certain ingroup or about issues associated with that ingroup often triggers use of verbal strategies associated with that group. Many native New Yorkers who live elsewhere report that when they talk about New York, especially with other New Yorkers, they find themselves using more features of New York style than usual. This is natural, because verbal devices, when shared, are part of what give people the feeling that they 'are on the same wave length'. It is the comfort and ease of using a shared communicative system that makes it pleasurable to talk to people of shared background, although the feeling may not be consciously attributed to that factor.

It is interesting to note that Sally mentioned that she 'loved' listening to a conversation like this one, even though it seemed strange to her. She lived with Steve for six years, so for her such conversation is associated with him. If she has positive feelings about that conversational style, those feelings necessarily come from her feelings about her history with Steve. Sally noted that when she first met Steve's family, their way of talking (i.e. exhibiting characteristics of the Columbus Circle discussion) was overwhelming to her, and a bit offensive. (One cannot help but recall here the split-screen scene from Woody Allen's film *Annie Hall,* contrasting the dinner talk of his New York hero and his midwestern heroine, exaggerated for comic effect.) But because of later positive associations, Sally now finds such conversation nostalgic. Attitudes toward speech styles are necessarily associated with attitudes toward the people one has met who exhibit those styles.[1]

Not everyone feels positive about people who use such conversational devices. An article in *New West* magazine (Esterly 1979) tells of the work of Gerald Goodman, a psychologist at the University of California, Los Angeles who believes that fast talkers are a conversational menace. He calls them 'crowders' (thus evincing his bias) and offers a training course (at a price) that is designed to help them learn 'patience'.

Goodman sees overlap and latching as obstructive moves: 'A slow talker may actually be allowed to end his thought, but then the other person immediately starts talking, and that contributes to a feeling of not being understood or appreciated or taken seriously. And, of course, if you get two aggressive, crowding people together in competition, there's a chain reaction and no communication' (p. 69). Goodman is expressing the view of the high-considerateness strategist. From another perspective, that of those operating on a high-involvement strategy, such as that demonstrated, the fact that interlocutors understand and appreciate each other is an assumption; the signaling load is on solidarity: showing interest and enthusiasm through fast pace.

Goodman's view, however, clearly expresses the perspective of many non 'crowders'. David and Sally were disconcerted by the rapid

---

[1]Note however the possibly patronizing and certainly distancing effect of the amused observer stance. It is rather like saying. 'Oh, aren't they cute?' (Thanks to R. Lakoff for pointing this out.)

pace and overlap that dominated the conversation, to the extent that it made it difficult for them to participate. David commented, 'I'm amazed at how you guys talk over each other—saying the same thing at the same time. When I have a conversation there are pauses.' David remarked that his parents often interrupted each other, but he had the feeling that this meant they wanted to block each other out. In this, he is expressing the popular view that Goodman holds of crowders: that overlap makes communication impossible. However, examples of the conversation at Thanksgiving dinner demonstrate that for some people overlap not only does not impede but in fact enhances communication.

Mutual Revelation

The Coliseum discussion contains yet another important phenomenon that is part of the conversational style of its participants. In (32) I make a statement about my own experience:

(32) Deborah I never <u>knew</u> where W I N S was.

Steve responds to this by making a statement about his experience:

(33)   Steve: That was my <u>haunt</u> cause I went down for children's
             concerts.

This is a device by which a personal statement is intended as a show of rapport. By this strategy, the speaker expects his or her statement of personal experience to elicit a similar statement from the other. Thematic cohesion is established by the metamessage: 'We are intimate; we both tell about ourselves; we are both interested in hearing about the other's experience'.

The effectiveness of this device is dependent upon the sharedness of the system. A friend told me about a disconcerting conversation she had with a man she had just met. During the conversation, the man regaled her with personal revelations about his past and his life. My friend could not help herself from asking him, 'Why are you telling me all this?' The man explained, 'Because I want to get to know you'. This seems at first (and seemed to her) patently absurd; how could he get to know HER by telling about HIMSELF? Yet his strategy makes sense if his personal revelations were intended as an invitation for her to follow suit. In fact, for one who shares such a system his revelations might be sensed as an imperative to follow suit, because resistance would be an obvious refusal to participate. He goes on and on, trying harder because she isn't doing her part.

The device of mutual revelation is part of a high-involvement style. It fits in with the image of conventionalized camaraderie that was illustrated in Chapter 1 in the example of the graduate student, who tried to establish rapport by asking a new acquaintance about her divorce. It also figures in a passage in the novel *Daniel Martin* by John Fowles. The narrator comments, with reference to an American couple seated at the protagonist's table on a cruise ship:

> The American pair seemed to have been abroad long enough—they had been in Cairo some four months—to have quelled that least attractive (to Dan) of national characteristics: the need to overwhelm you with personal information and then demand yours. The occasional conversation at lunch—it was properly a rectangular table for six, which allowed them some separation—was almost English in its generality. (pp. 506–7)

The preference for personal topics and the expectation of mutual revelation that the narrator associates with Americans comes from a high-involvement strategy for conventionalized camaraderie. The narrator of *Daniel Martin,* incidentally, is naive in his observation that the couple have given up what he calls an American 'national characteristic' because they have been abroad four months. It is highly unlikely that people would change strategies that quickly, if ever. It is more likely that the hero has come in contact with Americans who operate on a different strategy, one closer to his own, and closer to Chad's.

The strategy of trading personal statements need not be so dramatic as extended or deeply intimate revelations. It operates on a subtle level as well as in my comments and Steve's about W I N S, seen previously.

In this system, the interpersonal connection is the source of thematic cohesion. The rapport function—that is, the notion that because of our interpersonal connection we are interested in each other's revelations—is assumed. If such an assumption is not operative or if an interlocutor is not familiar with the mutual revelation device, then the most appropriate response to someone's personal statement would be a reaction to that stated condition or opinion. In other words, thematic cohesion would be established on the basis of content (hence the strategy is low on involvement). This is the strategy upon which Chad operated when I was trying to get him to talk about Goffman's work. Using the mutual revelation device, I said,

> I had never heard about him before I started studying linguistics.

This represents the same device that I used in my comment to Steve about WINS. I expected (and when I listen to the tape, I again expect) Chad to respond with a similar statement about himself, to tell me how he came across Goffman's work. Instead, Chad kept the focus on me:

> Chad: Really?
> Deborah: Yeah.

with the result that the interchange came to a temporary halt. Not surprisingly (knowing what we now know) the one who did pick up on my statement was Peter, who does just what I expected Chad to do: make a personal statement paralleling mine.

> Peter: That name is familiar but I don't I din know I didn't know
> anything about

Another extended interchange between Peter and me demonstrates the operation of mutual revelation. The discussion took place immediately after the Goffman discussion.

(1) Deborah: Do you réad? ....

(2)　　Peter: Do I réad? ...

(3) Deborah: Do you rèad things just for fún?

　　　　　　　　　　....

(4)　　Peter: Yeah. .... Right now I'm reading Norma Jean the
　　　　　　　　Térmite Queen.
　　　　　　　　[*laughs*]

(5) Deborah: ⌈Whàt's th́at? .... Norma Jean like uh: .... Marilyn
　　　　　　　ƒ
　　　　　　　Mon'róe?

(6)　　Peter: It's .. ‚No:. It's a book about ...... a housewife /??/
　　　　　　　　　　dec

(7) Deborah: Is it a ⌈nóvel or whàt.

(8)　　Peter: ˈÌt's a ‚nóvel.

(9) Deborah: 'Yeah?

(10)   Peter: Before that .... I read The French Lieutenant's Woman?
⌐Have you⌐read that?⌐
(11) Deborah: L Oh yeah?⌐ No. Whó wrote that?

(12)   Peter: John Fowles.

(13) Deborah: Yeah I've heárd that he's good.

(14)   Peter: 'He's a ∟gréat writer. 'Í think he's one of the ∟bést
           writers.⌐
        Deborah:⌐ hm

(15) Deborah: /?/

(16)   Peter: 'Hé's really ˌgoòd.

(17) Deborah: /?/

....

(18)   Peter: But Í get very bùsy. .... ⌐Y'know?
(19) Deborah: L Yeah. I- .. hàrdly eVer reàd.

....

(20)   Peter: What I've been dòing is cutting down on my sléep.
(21) Deborah: Oy!⌐ [*sighs*]
(22)   Peter: L And I've been [Steve *laughs*] ..... and I⌐s
(23) Deborah: Lí do that tòo
        but it's páinful.⌐
(24)   Peter: ⌐ Yeah. Fi:ve, six hours a 'níght,
       and⌐
(25) Deborah: ⌐ Oh Gód, hòw can you dó it. You survíve?

....

(26)   Peter: Yeah làte afternoon méetings are hàrd. .... But outside
                       Deborah: Lmmm⌐
        of thát I can keep gòing ⌐ pretty well
(27) Deborah: L Not sleeping enough is
        térrible .... I'd múch rather not eàt than not sleèp.
                              p
                         [Sally *laughs*]

(28)   Peter: I próbably should not èat so much, it would .. it
        would uh ... sáve a lot of tìme.

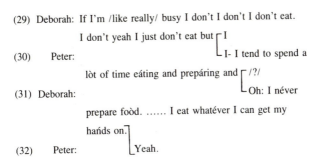

(29) Deborah: If I'm /like really/ busy I don't I don't I don't eat.
I don't yeah I just don't eat but ⌈I
(30)   Peter: ⌊I- I tend to spend a
lòt of time eáting and prepáring and ⌈/?/
(31) Deborah: ⌊Oh: I néver
prepare foòd. ...... I eat whatéver I can get my
hańds on.⌉
(32)   Peter: ⌊Yeah.

Peter and I exchange a series of mutual revelations about our own habits. With (19) I show that I understand what Peter means about being busy by saying that I hardly ever read (presumably because I am too busy). In (23) I say that I do the same, in response to his comment that he cuts down on sleep. I sympathize with his statement (26) about getting tired at late afternoon meetings by stating in (27) that I'd rather not eat than not sleep. In (28) Peter makes a comment about his eating habits, in (29) I describe mine, in (30) he reiterates his, and in (31) I reiterate mine. It might seem to some observers that we are not communicating at all, because we both persist in talking about ourselves. However, if one is familiar with the mutual revelation device, it is clear that we are showing our understanding of and concern for each other's statements by offering comparable personal statements.

Bonding Through High-Involvement Devices

Throughout Thanksgiving there is a significant amount of bonding between Peter and me. We listen to each other; we encourage each other to speak; we have a number of dyadic talks, or at least talks in which the main dynamic is between us. This is partly explainable by the fact that we have known each other for a significant length of time, although we have not been friends during that time in the sense that we have not socialized together much. It may also be attributable in part to the fact that we are both now single, in Peter's case recently so. But certainly the continuation of interchanges between us is at least in part due to the fact that our styles are rather similar, and therefore we find talk between us easy and satisfying.

There is evidence throughout the taped conversation, for example, that Peter and I use overlap in similar ways. This has been seen already, in the immediately preceding example. Peter and I both timed our comments to overlap with or immediately latch onto those of the other: Peter's comments (22), (24), and (30) and my (19), (23), (25), (27), and (31). Peter responds positively to my sudden focus of attention on his personal life. When I turn to him and ask (1) 'Do you read?' I use a rapid, abrupt question, introducing a new topic unexpectedly. After a brief hesitation in the form of restating my question (2) 'Do I read?' Peter not only answers the question but supplies specific information (4) about the book he is currently reading. That is, rather than just answering my sudden question as Chad did with 'Yeah', Peter volunteers added information that gives matter for further talk, the name of the book he is reading. I then ask him about the book, but it is apparent from (6) 'It's .. No: It's a book about ...... a housewife /??/' that Peter would have gone on to say more about it even if I had not asked. He begins by saying 'It's', then has to stop in order to answer my question with 'No', and then continues where he had started, with a sentence that now does double duty as a continuation of what he started to say and the answer to my question: 'It's a book about a housewife'. As with Steve in earlier examples, when I interrupt Peter in the middle of a sentence he wants to finish, he continues trying to say it until he succeeds. See, for example, (22) and (24), in which Peter makes three attempts to say that he sleeps only five or six hours a night.

When Peter finally says that he sleeps little, my response is swift: (25) 'Oh God, how can you do it. You survive?' Note the deletion of the auxiliary 'do' in 'You survive?' to render the reduced syntactic form of the question, a device discussed earlier.

Expressive Phonology and Intonation

An aspect of Peter's and my styles is expressive use of phonology and other paralinguistic cues. For example, my question (5) 'What's that?' is loud and high pitched. It will be seen in a later discussion that I use this device with Chad and David, with the result that they stop talking in surprise, wondering what caused my outburst. In the present segment, the high pitch on 'What's that?' is echoed in the way I end the question as well: The last syllable of 'Monroe' has very high pitch. It seems highly likely that my use of this pattern was triggered by Peter's self-mocking laughter as he finished saying the title of the book he was reading (4).

In responding to my exclamation (5), asking what the book is about,

Peter uses sharp contrasts in pitch and voice quality in (6) and (8) to signal the message, 'I know this is a silly book'. His pitch on (6), 'No', is very low, and he draws out the vowel, then utters the sentence with slowed pace. The effect of this tone quality is self-deprecating. The same signals function in (8) when he explains 'It's a novel'. Similar shifts from high to low pitch also function in Peter's evaluation of John Fowles:

(14)   Peter: 'Hé's a great writer. 'Í think he's one of the

          ˌbést writers.

(16)   Peter: 'Hé's really ˌgòod.

The pitch is very high on the beginnings of the sentences ['He's' in 'He's a great writer', and 'I' in 'I think' in (14); 'He's' in (16) 'He's really good'.]. The pitch is very low on the emphasized words at the ends of the sentences ['great writer' and 'best writers' in (14); 'good' in (16)]. The contour that results is repeated in all three statements and signals to me great earnestness and sincerity. Illustrated by lines, the intonational contours look like this:

When Peter says (20), that he has been cutting down on his sleep, I respond with a Yiddish language expression of suffering: (21) 'Oy!' I thus express sympathy for Peter's loss of sleep. My choice of a Yiddish 'response cry' (Goffman 1981) functions in a number of ways to establish rapport. First of all, I utter the cry as if it were an expression of my own feeling, thus taking Peter's point of view to show that I empathize with his feelings. Second, the fact that I chose a Yiddish expression signals, through metaphorical code-switching (Blom & Gumperz 1972), Peter's and my shared ethnic background. At the same time, however, the exaggerated nature of my response—the fact that I utter 'Oy!' with a great sigh—is a way of mocking my own usage, so that the utterance is ironic. The humor of this response is not lost on Steve, who has been engaged in a parallel conversation with other members of the group, but who, on hearing my exclamation, laughs loudly. (It will be seen, in the section on humor, that this type of self-mocking, stylized ironic usage is typical of Steve's own humor, and that I am his best audience when he employs it.)

I continue the device of expressing exaggerated concern for Peter's loss of sleep in (23), (25), and (27). These comments are all spoken with marked stress and breathy voice quality that express exaggerated and stylized concern. The entire interchange, thus, exhibits marked pitch shifts and exaggerated stress, which gives it a sense of expressiveness and empathy (to Peter and me).

My interchange with Peter ends with observations about dating. Peter volunteers the information that following his separation, he went through a period of dating a lot, but now he has decided that he does not find that satisfying. I make a generalization (a device typical of my style) to the effect that his experience is 'normal'. At the end of our exchange, both the rhythm and content of our comments effect harmony and conclusion:

(1) Deborah: Well that's a véry usual páttern. I mean I think when you suddenly

find yourself single, of cóurse what you want to do is date a

lot. …. In fact I would think it would s remain interesting for about

a yéar. [*laugh*] Thén you get borèd.

….

(2)   Peter: We:ll, I thínk I got bòred. [Deborah *laughs*] Well I-I
                        acc

mean basically what I feel is what I really líke …

is péople. And getting to know them réally wéll. And

you just cán't get to know …. <u>ten</u> people <u>really</u>
                                 [*breathy*]

<u>well</u>. ⌜You can't dó it.
             │   *p*
(3) Deborah: ⌞Yeah right. Y'have to there's no- Yeah

there's ⌜no tíme.
(4)   Peter: ⌞There's not tíme.
(5) Deborah: Yeah …. 'strue.

At the beginning of (2), Peter takes my words 'Then you get bored', and restates them. By pausing, and by contrasting the drawn-out 'well' with the clipped, fast 'I think I got bored', he creates a humorous effect. He uses pauses to highlight the key words 'people' and 'ten'. The word 'ten' is also emphasized by breathy voice quality, and the words 'really well' are also uttered, the second time, with a plosive emphasis. Peter's statements (2) and (4) flow in a continuous stream, ending with 'You can't do it. There's not time'. However the phrase 'There's not time' echoes my words in (3). My 'Yeah .... 'strue' in (5) marks the agreement that seals the discussion. The end of the talk is also signaled by the quieting down of the tone; our voices are softer; our talk is slower. It is like a fade-out.

Persistence

Throughout the Thanksgiving dinner, our conversational behavior shows that Peter and Steve and I operate on the assumptions that if someone wants to say something, s/he will find the time to say it. By this system, the burden of the speaker is not to make room for others to speak nor to ascertain whether others want to hear one's comments. Rather, the conversationalist's burden is to maintain a show of rapport by offering comments. That others will want to hear whatever comments one has to make, is taken as given. The fact that one makes this assumption is in itself a show of rapport. Similarly, one assumes that others know that one is interested in hearing whatever comments they may have.

Thus, one of the characteristics of our style is that Peter and I persist when we have something to say. This has already been seen in some of the preceding examples. Both Peter and I persist with contributions for two, three, and four tries. For example, in the following segment, I am explaining a paper in which I have written about differences in conversational pace. I have told Sally that she has appeared as an example in a paper I wrote (Tannen 1975), and I am explaining the difference between Sally's and my turn-taking styles, as discussed in that paper:

(1) Deborah: u:m .. That Sally would .. was .. was sort of had learned →
        Steve: ⌊ / ? / was waiting   / ? / ⌋

     Deborah: to wait for a moment of silence before making a contribution, →
        Steve: ⌊/cutting/ everything off before she   /?/⌋

     Deborah: .... and I- was taught to never let there <u>be</u> any

             silence. ..... So I would jump in. [*laughs*]

             [*laughter*]

                  .....

→ (2)   Peter: That's really

(3) Deborah: ⌐Dju /?/- ⌐Did you-⌐Dídn't I tell you that ⌐I wrote that→

→ (4)   Peter: └⌐Í noticed

                         ⌐that ....

           Deborah: └paper? ⌐Oh yeah. *[laughs]*

→ (5)   Peter: ⌐Actually Í noticed that balance a lót .. with people.

(6) Deborah: └I should send you a copy.

                 Sally: └Yeah.⌡

                    .....

→ (7)   Peter: Y'know there are sòme people I have to be véry verbally aggrèssive with cause they never <u>let</u> ... a moment of silence devélop, and other people, /?/

Peter begins his comment four times, the first three timed to overlap with my talk. The first three tries, (2), (4), and (5) fail because I do not stop for him. By (7), however, I have finished my conversation with Sally about the paper in which I mention her, and therefore Peter succeeds in making his comment. It is amusing that Peter is illustrating the very phenomenon he is (and I am) talking about. That is, he has to be 'very verbally aggressive' at that moment, because I am the sort of person he is (and I have just been) referring to, who does not LET a moment of silence develop.

At yet another point in the conversation, Peter makes four tries before he gets the floor. In this case, there is much simultaneous talk as people are sitting down to dinner. Peter tells a joke:

(1)   Steve: So should we ⌐dó that? ⌐Should we start with the ⌐white

             Deborah: └Sure⌝

→ (2)   Peter: └Didju hear

             about the- .. ⌐lady, who was asked,

(3) Deborah: └I'm gonna get in there, right?

(4)   Chad: Okay.

→ (5)   Peter: Didju 'hear?

(6)   David: Wè have to sit bóy girl boy.

(7)   Chad: Bòy girl bóy?

→ (8)   Peter: Didju hear about the lady who was àsked,

(9)   Chad: └ There's only two girls ⌡

(10) Deborah: What?

→(11)   Peter: Did you hear about the lady who was ásked ... Do you→
          dec   Chad: ⌊Boy girl boy⌋

         smoke after sèx?

(12)   David: I don't knów I never loóked. [*nasal tone*]

(13) Deborah: And she said? What?

(14)   Peter: I don't <u>know</u> I never ⌈'<u>looked.</u>

(15) Deborah: ⌊Oh [*chuckles*]

Peter attempts to begin his joke in (2), (5), and (8) before he finally gets to tell it in (11), because everyone else is concerned with sitting down to dinner. Steve is talking about the wine (1) and the rest of us are talking about seating arrangements. When Peter finally begins his joke (11) with audience attention, David supplies the punchline (12) in a nasal, twangy voice that is disguised to mimic the speaker in the joke. There is no evidence that Peter is disconcerted by the obstructions to his joke telling, nor that he hesitates about whether to tell it once he has made up his mind to do so, despite what might be taken as lack of interest from the others. Peter's only adjustment is a slight deceleration and overarticulation in (11) when he pronounces 'Did you hear about the <u>lady who was asked</u>,' and a noticeably emphatic tone in (14) when he repeats the punchline. These do not sound annoyed, only emphasized.

Following is an example in which I persist with a comment I wish to introduce. The topic of discussion has been Chad's participation in the cross-country whistle-stop tour sponsored by the production studio he works for. David remarks (boasting for Chad in a way that friends frequently do) that Chad may get to make a similar trip through Europe.

(1)   David: Y'know they might get to go to Eúrope? ..... And do the
           same thing in Eúrope? In the spríng?

(2)   Peter: Oh really.⌉

(3) Deborah: ⌊Really.⌉

(4)   Steve: ⌊Oh:.
                  f

(5)   Peter: Thát sounds like fùn.

→ (6) Deborah: ⌈Did

(7)   Chad: ⌊ And take the tráin tour through Eùrope.

→ (8) Deborah: Did yóu .. ⌈ serve a function

(9)   Peter: ⌊ Except wouldn't it it be nice if you had a
                   acc

        little more tíme there?

(10) Chad: Yeah- We:ll we /?? / discovered that. ... But we
also know .. we found out we .. found out the mán who
owned all the .. the who bóught all the càrs from the
Órient Expréss. .... So we'll got all .. gèt all the
old cars from the Órient Expréss and stìck them all
    [Deborah *chuckles*]
together. ..... and take it.
  p

(11) Steve: ⌐What was the Órient Exprèss?

→(12) Deborah: ⌐Were yóu serving a fùnction on the tour, or did you
just get to go alóng.

(13) Chad: I was just invited along. ... It was rĥy idéa and
things like that y'know cause I wórked on the shòw.
p, acc - - - - - - - -]

I try to start my question in (6) and (8) but am superseded by Chad
(7) and then Peter (9). I finally ask the question in (12), this time not
giving in to Steve's competing question (11). (There is a balance in
Steve's and my alternating interruptions of each other.)

On another occasion, when the meal is finished and things are being
cleared away, Peter makes three attempts to bring up the topic of des-
sert. None of them is responded to, so he drops the matter.

Such examples of speaker persistence are not found in the speech of
Sally, David, or Chad. They do not persist more than two tries. For
example, the following segment represents the most 'aggressive' try
Sally makes during the dinner conversation. Steve and I were questioning David about sign language. Our discussion began with Steve asking
David how to say *discrete* in sign language. Several turns later Sally
asks David how he said *discrete,* but David is still busy answering
another question that was posed by Steve and me. Rather than continue
to try to get David's attention, Sally turns to someone else to pursue her
question. At that point, David does direct himself to her to answer, but
he does not really give her the information she requests. Nonetheless,
she lets the matter drop.

(1) David: No. I don't think si- ... No. I don't think Víctor
   Deborah: ⌐ They don't?⌐

would .. ever sáy that.
   Deborah: ⌐ Huh? ⌐

(2) Sally: What what what was discréte?
  p

(3) David: You'd use thís. Inform. Inform. [*making sign*]

(4) Sally: Did he tell us what discréte was?
                     p

(5) David: u:m, dis u:m ... There's different ... wa- there's
                                              Peter: ⌐uhuh⌐

        different ⌐ways of talking about it.
(6) Peter: ⌐Are there díctionaries of sign?
                     p

(7) David: Yeah.

Following is an extended segment of the dinner conversation in which Steve, Peter, and I all simultaneously persist in talking about our own topics, with little or no response from anyone. This segment occurs while we are eating.

(1) Deborah: Í wònder how óur ... ⌐grándparents and párents fèlt
(2) Peter: /?/   ⌐cranberry sauce. ⌐
                about Thanks'gìving.

(3) Peter: Cránberry sauce.

(4) Deborah: It wàsn't their hóliday.

(5) Peter: It's a wónderful hóliday.

                     .....

(6) Peter: Is that the cranberry sauce?
                     p, acc
(7) Deborah: I wónder if they díd it⌐
(8) Chad: ⌐One holiday a year for stuff
        ⌐for stuffing yourself?
(9) Peter: ⌐Y'know what we should really have?
(10) Steve: Could ⌐wé get this off the tàble?⌐
(11) Deborah: ⌐/ ?   / ⌐→
                Y'know if they used to do it for the kíds, or whether→
(12) Peter: ⌐I'd like if off→
        Deborah: they really félt it.
        Peter: the table⌐
(13) Steve: It kéeps coming back on the 'tàble. It múst have a
        will of its ‚òwn.→
        ⌐That's all Í can say. [*clipped tone throughout*]
(14) Peter: ⌐We should have more nàpkins.

```
(15)    Steve:  uh- well,⌐
(16)    Sally:          ⌊Stéve's parents ... féel it. ... Théy feel,
                ... réally strongly⌐
(17)    Steve:                   ⌊⌐Súre they do. ⌐Yeah, it's a màjor
                uh ....
(18)    Peter:  It's álways been my fàvorite hòliday.
(19) Deborah:   Well I wonder how⌐
(20)    Peter:                   ⌊except maybe for ..⌐Pésach
(21) Deborah:                                       ⌊Well yóur
                paren- théir parents were born in this coùntry.
(22)    Sally:  Yeah.
(23) Deborah:   But my parents⌐
(24)    Peter:  [to Chad]      ⌊⌐Are yóu Jewish?  Yóu're not Jewish.
                acc------------------------------------------------------]
```

I introduce the topic (1) of how 'our grandparents and parents felt
about Thanksgiving', since they were immigrants to the United States.
In making this statement, incidentally, I am bonding with Peter and
Steve, and possibly Chad, to the exclusion of David, whose parents and
grandparents were born in this country, and Sally, who is British.
(Much earlier I addressed the same question to her, asking whether she
had 'internalized' Thanksgiving as a holiday.) In this sense, my bring-
ing up the topic again is in itself a form of persistence with a topic of
interest to me. I pursue this topic over seven turns, in (1), (4), (7), (11),
(19), (21), (23). I continue trying to make my point, as others either
ignore my topic or respond to it in a way that I feel misses my point.
During the same conversational segment, Peter talks about the food
over five turns: three concerned with cranberry sauce, (2), (3), (6), and
two with napkins, (9), (14), none of which elicits any response from
others. Steve, for his part, takes two turns about the tape recorder (10),
(13), also unintegrated into others' talk.

Peter's remark (5) 'It's a wonderful holiday' appears to be a response to my second try (4) 'It wasn't their holiday'. Paralinguistically,
it echoes the sound and rhythm of my comment in an almost poetic way.
His choice of the word 'wonderful' echoes my verb 'wonder', and the
sound of 'wonderful' echoes the initial consonant and the rhythm of my
'wasn't their.' (Sacks [1971] noted the tendency of speakers to choose
words just used by interlocutors or that use sounds that appeared immediately prior. He called that process 'sound selection' or 'sound touch-

offs'.) However, although Peter's response (5) coheres with the rhythm and topic of my remark (4), it does not cohere with my comment. Whereas I am making a point about the feeling of immigrants for the holidays of their new country, Peter says something about his own feelings for Thanksgiving.[2] He does this again in (18) 'It's always been my favorite holiday'. Peter is employing the strategy I have discussed previously of making a personal statement as a conversational contribution. However, I have not been making personal statements, but rather have been trying to elicit a theoretical discussion. Therefore, I am not satisfied with his contribution and persist in trying to get the conversation to focus on the topic as I see it.

The one who picks up on my point most closely is Sally in (16) 'Steve's parents feel it. They feel really strongly'. It is clear that Sally is answering my question, because she uses the expression 'feel it' that I use in (1) and repeat in (11). Sally's remark (16) directly answers my question about how our parents felt about Thanksgiving. However, there is an ambiguity in my use of the phrase 'grandparents and parents'. What I meant was 'my parents and your grandparents,' i.e. those who came to the United States as immigrants. Because Steve's parents were born in the United States, my question does not apply to them. However, in responding, Steve picks up the focus of Sally's remark, not my initial question. Peter, however, is still on his own tack, expressing his feelings about the holiday in (18) and (20).

I continue trying to explain what I had in mind in (21) and (23), but I am finally cut off by Peter, who turns to Chad with a new question as well as a projected response to it: (24) 'Are you Jewish? You're not Jewish'. Peter asks this in just the way that I asked questions of Chad in segments discussed earlier—suddenly focusing on him personally. It is easy to see what led Peter to this question. His comment about his feelings about holidays led him from Thanksgiving to a Jewish holiday, Pesach (Passover) in (20), and this led him to wonder whether Chad was Jewish. Chad answers, I do not hear his answer correctly, there ensues a discussion about my hearing, and then the conversation turns to the food. My observation about immigrants and Thanksgiving is never picked up.

In this segment, then, I persisted over seven turns in attempts to make a point. Peter pursued other points over five turns, responded to

---

[2]Robin Lakoff points out that Peter may have taken my comment as an implicit criticism of Thanksgiving—i.e. 'not a holiday for everyone'—and be contradicting that. Nonetheless, his comment does not build on my point as I intend it.

my remark without responding to my point twice, and finally turned the discussion off my topic entirely. Steve pursued his own preoccupation with keeping the table attractive, with only a brief ratification from Peter, (12). No one else acknowledged his remarks at all, and no one moved the tape recorder.

Tolerance for Noise vs. Silence

Thus, Peter, Steve, and I pursue our own interests in talk. When Chad says something, (8) 'One holiday a year for stuffing yourself', he is responding to Peter's remark. Sally's comment (16) responds to mine. They do not toss out new, unrelated ideas of their own, simply because they thought of them. The overall effect of three speakers all persisting with their own topics is a period of diffuse talk.

A concomitant of the persistence device, and the assumption that one's thoughts are of interest, is a tolerance for such distraction and diffuse talk, which is related to the tolerance for overlap. When Sally, David, and Chad listened to this segment on tape, they noted that it sounded odd (to say the least) to hear Steve, Peter, and me pursuing different topics at the same time. Chad volunteered that his conversations tend to stick to one topic at a time. In contrast, it sounds natural to Steve, Peter, and me for various topics to be tossed about until one is picked up and developed. Such simultaneous raising of topics is a necessary outgrowth of the assumption that it is appropriate for speakers to introduce new topics just because they thought of them, and that a topic should not necessarily be dropped simply because it was not picked up on the first few tries.

What speakers of this system cannot tolerate is the alternative to this strategy: silence. That is, if speakers do not toss out whatever comes into their heads, and if topics are dropped after one or two tries, there will necessarily be periods of silence in conversation between topics. In fact, it is likely that many of the devices of the high-involvement system found in this conversation grow out of intolerance for silence. This opposition is noted by Goodman as well: 'It may come as a bulletin to crowders that one of their options is S-I-L-E-N-C-E'. Again, John Fowles notes this aspect of contrast between communicative strategies of American and British speakers. In *Daniel Martin*, the protagonist, who has been living in California, visits his native England and immediately violates the rules on a British train:

When we drew out of the station the elderly woman opposite me glanced up at the ventilation window. It was slightly open. A minute later she glanced again. I said, 'Shall I shut it?'

'Oh well if ...'

I stood and shut it; and received a frozen grimace, meant to represent gratitude, from the lady and two or three covertly disapproving examinations from my male fellowpassengers. I had committed the cardinal sin not of shutting the window, but of opening my mouth. No other caste in the world [are] so certain that public decency and good breeding is silence ... (139).

The system described by Fowles is the polar opposite of that exhibited by Steve, Peter, and me in the Thanksgiving talk: one system seeks comfort in interaction, the other in silence. The fact that Sally grew up in the environment Fowles is describing may have something to do with the fact that she is the most silent of the members of the Thanksgiving dinner.[3]

Thus the participants in the Thanksgiving dinner conversation showed different expectations with respect to what is appropriate to say and how it is appropriate to say it. Steve, Peter, and I shared the tendency to feel comfortable with personal topics of talk. We showed interest by asking machine-gun questions, and we used marked shifts in pitch and amplitude to show expressiveness and enthusiasm. In addition, we used overlap and fast pacing as cooperative devices, contributing to the enthusiasm effect. We operated on a strategy that puts the signaling load on involvement. For example, we assumed that irrelevant topics were of interest because we thought of them, and we persisted in our introduction of topics far longer than did the other speakers. Thus we showed a high tolerance for noise and diffuse topics as opposed to silence. All these devices operated to give the conversation its 'frenetic' tone, and to establish among us a sense of rapport and successful communication.

The other members of the group, David, Chad, and Sally, did not participate in the use of these devices. During the interchanges in which Steve, Peter, and I used them, the other members were silent or par-

---

[3]Basso (1979) has documented the positive view of silence for Western Apaches, as has Scollon (in press) for northern Athabaskans. The issue of the cross-cultural significance of silence is a particularly rich one and is treated from a number of perspectives in papers collected in Tannen and Saville-Troike (in press). The basic issue, perhaps, is that there are cross-cultural differences in expectations about when a pause becomes a silence, and when interlexical juncture becomes a pause.

ticipating minimally. In dyadic interchanges with Chad, I clearly vio-
lated his expectations about topic and pace, and David and Sally remarked during playback that the fast, expressive, overlapping
conversation seemed odd to them. Their lack of experience with such
devices made it difficult for them to participate.

CHAPTER 5

Narrative Strategies

Integrally related to expectations about pace, overlap, rate of speech, and other conversational devices that have been discussed are expectations about the telling of narratives in conversation. All of these devices operate in the telling of stories just as they do in other forms of talk, but in addition, there are verbal devices that are specific to the telling of stories.

Narrative is not a discrete category but a prototype. Some verbal texts are more narrative than others. The prototypical narrative, or story (I will use these terms interchangeably), recounts events that occurred in the past. However, there are numerous instances of talk that resemble narrative in some ways but not in others. For example, during the Thanksgiving conversation, Peter summarized an article he had read in a sociology journal about adopted children, and Chad at one point described Victor signing. Neither of these accounts seemed quite like narratives because they did not recount events. At first, Chad's seemed more narrative in that it told about something he had seen. But Chad referred to Victor in order to justify a point he was making about the difference between sign and spoken language, and his listeners reacted not to his experience but to his observation about language. Thus, Peter's summary of the article he had read more closely resembled a narrative, because it triggered a series of stories about adopted children. However, I did not count either of these accounts as narratives. In order to isolate a certain segment of the data for analysis, I decided to consid-

Table 1 Use of Narratives in Thanksgiving Conversation

Name	Total number of turns	Total number of narratives told	Total number of narrative turns	Average number of words per narrative turn	Percentage of turns which are narrative	Average number of words per narrative	Number of stories told in clusters
Steve	594	15	36	23	6%	46	8
Deborah	811	13	21	45	3%	80	5
Peter	417	8	16	40	4%	81	6
Chad	405	4	8	47	2%	94	0
David	386	4	18	34	5%	154	2
Sally	169	4	8	21	5%	43	0

er *stories* only those accounts that adhered to the strictest definition, that is, those that told about past events.

In all, 48 clearly identifiable narratives were told during the dinner conversation. There are significant differences in the number of narratives told by different members of the group (see Table 1). Steve told the most (15); I was a close second (13); Peter came next (8); Chad, David, and Sally told fewer (4 each). This hierarchy corresponds to the sense that most of the participants reported, that Steve was the most 'dominant' participant, followed by me and then Peter, whereas Chad, David and Sally participated much less.

Because some participants spoke more than others, the sheer numbers of narratives told may be misleading. Therefore, I calculated the number of narrative turns as a percentage of the total number of turns spoken by each participant (see Table 1). This yields slightly different results. Steve still emerges as the one most given to storytelling, with 6 percent of his turns devoted to narratives. However, David and Sally are close to him, with 5 percent of their talk devoted to narrative. This contrasts with the fact that David and Sally are the two participants who spoke the least number of turns during the conversation. Furthermore, Peter and I switch places with respect to percentage of talk devoted to storytelling (Peter 4 percent and I, 3 percent). Chad is the speaker least given to narrative talk; only 2 percent of his turns are devoted to telling stories.

Looked at in connection with other aspects of storytelling, these statistics are revealing. For example, the low percentage of narrative turns in Chad's talk correlates with his observable reluctance to volunteer information about his personal experiences. Thus, he tells three of his four narratives in answer to direct questions by others. (The fourth is about a cartoon strip he read as a child.) Chad is the only speaker in the group who is directly questioned in this way.

I tell 13 stories during the conversation. The most striking fact about them is that 7 of the 13 are told in support of someone else's point or matching someone else's story. In contrast, Steve tells three stories that contradict someone else's point, and, even more uniquely, 8 of his stories either offer his own experience, unasked or even unrelated to what has been going on before, or explain some reference or remark that he himself made immediately prior to the narrative. This may have contributed to the impression Peter reported that Steve had somehow 'dominated' the gathering.

It is interesting that Steve and Sally tell the shortest stories, on the average, and they have, on the average, the smallest number of words per turn. Steve's narrative turns contain an average of 23 words and Sally's 21; his narratives have an average of 46 words each, and Sally's 43. Thus while Steve tells a lot of stories, the stories he tells are comparatively short. His storytelling style is succinct. He does not give long orientations or explanations. Sally's stories are understated. But despite that (or because of that) she has a hard time getting the point of her stories across to this group.

Peter's stories are all personal, and half of them are about his children. Furthermore, Peter is particularly apt to tell stories in a round.

Story Rounds

One way in which stories function in the Thanksgiving conversation is in story rounds. Ethnomethodologists note that stories in conversation are often told in clusters or sequences (Ryave 1978). However, I use the term *story round* to refer to a particular kind of story cluster, in which speakers exchange stories of personal experiences that illustrate similar points. The stories told in rounds during Thanksgiving differ in some ways from the stories told in other contexts. For one thing, they require little or no orientation section; that is, the speaker does not begin by introducing the story with something like 'Did I tell you what happened . . .' or 'You'll never guess what happened . . .' The very juxtaposition of stories furnishes thematic cohesion. (See for example stories presented on pp. 111 and 113.)

21 of the 48 stories told during Thanksgiving dinner were told in a total of five rounds. The first round consisted of 3 stories about sex differences in language; the second round was made up of 5 stories about people the speakers knew who were adopted; the third round, of 5 stories about summer camp; the fourth round of 5 stories about freak accidents; the last round, of 4 stories about children and sex. (There was at least one more story told in this round, but the tape ran out shortly after I began it, so it is not included in the analysis.)

The story round device clearly belongs to the high-involvement strategy members of the group. Nineteen of the 21 stories told in rounds were told by Steve, Peter, and me. Chad and Sally told not a single story in a round. In contrast, 6 of Peter's 8 stories were told in rounds.

The story round is another example of the failure of purely surface phenomena to elucidate what is going on in interaction, in this case, to show the difference between a story cluster and a story round. Just as overlap is a surface phenomenon whereas interruption is an interpretive category (Bennett 1978a), so a story cluster is identifiable simply by reference to the contiguity of stories in conversation, but the existence of a round requires the establishment of thematic cohesion in an appropriate way. For example, David's participation in the story rounds yields different results from those of the other three.

Contrastive Narrative Strategies

An examination of David's four stories supports his recollection that he had been able either to be the center of attention or to observe the interaction but not to 'be part of the flow.' His stories, on the average, were strikingly long: an average of 154 words each (see Table 1). This length is not approached by anyone else. One effect of telling long stories is to keep the speaker the center of attention.

David's longest story is one in which he tells about an episode on a television program. Ostensibly, this story is part of a story round about adopted children. The round was triggered by Peter's summary of the article he had read reporting research to the effect that the children of adopted parents have IQ's closer to those of their natural parents than their adoptive parents. Steve immediately offered a story about a student and then another about a friend who were adopted and were very different from their adoptive parents. David followed with a story about some cousins of his who were adopted. (This story will be presented later.) I then told about a friend of Steve's and mine who is adopted and 'sticks out' in his family; Steve comments on my story by saying:

> Steve: Y'mean just because he TALKS LIKE THIS. But 'ánybody
> who tàlked like thát would stick out like a sòre thùmb.

In saying this, Steve mimics the friend in question by speaking in a loud, nasal, and rasping voice. Several turns later he says, seriously, 'He's just very <u>loud</u>'.

At that point, David begins a story about a satirical sketch he saw on the television program 'Saturday Night Live':

(1)   Steve: He <u>does</u> look different? He's just very <u>loud</u>.

(2)   David: Speaking of which they had the Lóud family. Remember
                                      [Deborah *laughs*]

            the Lóud family? On Sàturday Night Líve?

(3)   Steve: What was the Lóud family?

(4)   David: Dju hear about that? THEY TALK LIKE THIS.

       p

       [*laughter*]

(5)   Steve: I know lóts of people in New York who talk like thàt.

(6) Deborah: ⌐ You don't .. yknow the Loud family.

(7)   David: └ / ??   / the Loud family.⌐

(8)   Steve: └Are they all

(9) Deborah: It was a thing on télevision called An American Fámily.

There ensues a brief discussion explaining that the Loud family had been the subject of a TV documentary. When everyone is agreed upon who they were, David tries to begin his story again, but there is still confusion about what they have to do with the television program David has referred to:

(10)   David: So they had the⌐ Loud family.

(11)   Peter: └ So they're gonna be on? The whole

        family's, gonna be on?

(12) Deborah: Where.

(13)   Peter: The .. Saturday Night Live?

(14) Deborah: ⌐ No. No. /?/

(15)   David: └ No, last week they had the LOUD family. On Saturday

        Night Live. And it's like ... and the and the parents

        are <u>trying to</u> FIGURE OUT ... WHY THEIR KIDS, ... just

        ALIENATE, ...

David then proceeded to tell about the satirical sketch in which a family named Loud constantly yelled at each other, without realizing that they were doing so.

The connection between David's story and the one preceding it is the reference to people who are loud. Like Steve, David imitates the loud speech in his narrative. Steve's 'SHE TALKS LIKE THIS' is echoed by David's (4) 'THEY TALK LIKE THIS'. However, there is a problem with thematic cohesion. David has a lot of trouble with his orientation section before he can launch his narrative. Peter and Steve are both confused and ask a series of questions showing misunderstanding (3) (8) (11) (13), before they grasp what David's story is about. David finally goes ahead with his story (15) without explaining to Peter that it is not the Loud family themselves but a satire about them that he is telling about. Presumably, Peter caught on while the story was being told.

After David tells this extended story, recounting the details of the television episode, I comment, 'All on the pun of Loud, huh.' In a subtle way, my comment is (though was not consciously intended to be) a censure; it is as if to say the story was too long to illustrate a pun. In addition, it seems to betray my feeling that the connection by pun is not sufficient to warrant inclusion in the round. Thematic cohesion is established in rounds through the stories having similar or opposing points.

Nonetheless, David is the only non-New Yorker who participates in story rounds at all. On two occasions, he contributes stories to rounds that do cohere in an appropriate way. However, there are some other differences that emerge in terms of pace and formulating the points of the stories.

Following is a narrative that David told with Chad's participation. In the immediately preceding conversation, I have been talking about men's and women's language and have told about an upcoming lecture by a woman who teaches men who are about to undergo sex-change operations how to talk like women. After general exclamations about and reactions to this announcement, David tells about a conversation that he and Chad had the night before with a friend of theirs named Randy. David's story is about sexual orientation and voice quality, and therefore it is appropriately coherent with the topic of the round. There is much interest among the group members in David's story. However, there is evidence that some of the other members of the group expected stories to be told somewhat differently from the way David (with the help of Chad) was telling it.

It becomes clear that I felt David and Chad did not get to the point of their story quickly enough. This can be seen in my repeated questions that serve to prompt them to tell the point. (Overlapping talk by Steve and Peter is occasioned by the timer going off in the kitchen during this interchange.)

(1) David: Well ... what was Rándy saying last níght? ... He was
              talking about y'know he works <u>Ran</u>dy works at
              the uh [name of firm]? At ... [place of firm]? ....
              Chad: └ Right ┘
              Something he works with chíldren? .... Lánguage
              development? ┐   *p*

(2) Chad: └ Yeah he he does .. lánguage evaluation

on ... autìstic a:nd .. all those .. kind of children.

David: └Yeah ┘

[*timer goes off in kitchen*]

(3)   David: Crazy children.┐

(4)   Steve: ┌What time is it Peter?

→(5) Deborah: └So what was he sáying.

(6)   Chad: He was talking about┐

(7)   Peter: └Twenty-five till

(8)   Steve: ┌Twenty-five to?

(9)   Chad: └There was a there was a

(10)   David: There was a <u>staff conference</u>

(11)   Chad: Right. A staff conference.

(12)   David: And they were ... these incredible, ... these

              psychiatrists? ... got up there? ....

              Chad: └mhm┘   *p*   Steve: [*chuckles*] hm

→(13) Deborah: Whát were they doing.

(14)   Peter: [*from kitchen*] Steve you're having /?/ problems back here.

(15)   Chad: Well they were talking about séxual idéntity and all

              this kind of stuff. So this ... óne woman was┐

(16)   David: └One

              woman was talking about .. the gáy voíce.

              Steve: └/?/ ┘

(17)   Chad: Yeah the gáy voìce. She was talking about gáy voìces.

              David: └The gay voice┘

(18)   David: And <u>Ran</u>dy was sitting there <u>simm</u>ering.

(19)   Chad: Right. ┌/?/

→(20) Deborah: └Whát was he 'sáying.

(21)   Chad: They were wondering whether or not it was .. hormónal.

(22)   David: Whether the ┌<u>gay</u> voice was hormonal.

(23) Deborah: └'WHAT!┘

                           ff

(24)   Chad: Yeah. Whether the gáy voice was hormònal.┐

(25) Deborah: └You're kidding! ┘

                  ......

(26) Deborah: Wo:w.

                 .....

(27)   Steve: Oh God!
                 p

                      ....

(28)   Chad: Or whether it was leárned behavior, or was w whether

               it was ... uh <u>learned</u> behavior, o:r genetic, or

               hormonal or what. ⌐ /? as they were gonna/
(29)   Steve: ⌊ Ooo that makes my skín creep. .... ew:
                                  p,dec

In listening to this conversation on tape, I reexperienced my impatience with David and Chad for not getting to the point that Randy had been present at a meeting at which discussants suggested that the 'gay voice was hormonal.' Three times I ask questions to prompt David and Chad to get to the point:

    (5) So what was he sáying.

    (13) Whát were they doing.

    (20) Whát was he 'sáying?

The first two questions do not necessarily show impatience. I offer such prompts to other storytellers as well. However, the third prompt (20) clearly shows impatience, in the raised pitch on the stressed word 'saying'. I have played this segment to others of backgrounds similar to mine, and they have remarked (without prompting from me) that David and Chad are having a hard time getting to the point of their story. During playback, David noticed my questions as well. I was surprised, however, at his explanation of what was going on.

David noted first that he began his story in a 'weak' way:

(1)   David: Well ... what was Rándy saying last night? ... He was

               talking about y'know he works <u>Ran</u>dy works at

               the .. uh [name of firm]? At ... [place of firm]?
               Chad: ⌊ right ⌐

               .... Something he works with chíldren? .... Lánguage
                                                                  p
               development?

David pointed out that he started with 'Well', then paused, and generally sounded as if he was not very sure of what he was saying. Although

David did not say so, the unsureness comes also from the filler ('uh'), the repeated pauses, false starts, and the question intonation at the ends of phrases. David said that he was hesitant first because he was not sure people would want to hear the story. Second he said that, although he knows perfectly well what Randy does, yet he spoke as if he did not and looked to Chad for confirmation, to cover himself, lest Chad contradict him. Finally, he wanted to draw Chad into the conversation, since Chad was David's guest and friend and David felt 'paternalistic' toward him in this setting. Chad, on the other hand, recalled that he was hesitant because it was really David's story, and he too was wary lest he make an error that David would then contradict.

In addition, David said that he was fishing for just the sort of encouragement that I supplied with my questions. These questions were reassurance to him that his story was of interest. David noted, however, that he did pick up a slight sense of impatience in my tone, and that that might have reinforced his hesitance. Chad independently noted the same phenomenon during playback. He remarked that had I not asked any prompting questions, he might well have discontinued the story. However, coming as they did, my questions made him wonder what I wanted, which then made him feel hesitant about saying anything, hence the tentative sense of his narrative. Thus, both David and Chad were, operating on defensive strategies, preferring to err by saying less, whereas Steve and I would sooner risk error by saying more.

David also pointed out, with characteristic perceptiveness about language processes, that at the same time that I asked (13) 'What were they doing?' Steve uttered the sound 'hm' in a way that David recognized as characteristic of Steve and synonymous with my question. That is, David hit upon the notion of pragmatic synonymy. Steve's 'hm' was also a way of encouraging David to go on while evidencing some impatience. David said it sounds to him as if Steve is holding himself back, forcing himself to be patient with David's slower pace.

David's idea of telling a story presupposes a certain hesitancy. It is appropriate, he explained, to give an indication of what one has to say and then see if anyone picks up on it, rather than imposing the story whether others like it or not. However, David's strategy is exaggerated in this interchange. Feeling a bit insecure in the setting, he begins his story even more hesitantly than he otherwise might have. This increased hesitance then arouses Steve's and my impatience, and the evidence of our impatience reinforces his feeling that he is not fitting in very well. In other words, we have a situation of complementary schismogenesis.

Expressive vs. Understated Evaluation and Response

David explained another peculiarity of this interchange as well. After (24), when David and Chad have told the point of their story (about the gay voice being hormonal), there is a series of pauses in the conversation. After a two-second pause, I say (26) 'Wo:w', and after another pause of a second and a half, Steve says (27), 'Oh God!' Both Steve and I (recalling Sally's characterization of us as 'a two-man team') fill the pauses with loud and marked exclamations in response to David's story. David noted that he did not think that would have happened if it had been one of us telling the story. My first reaction was to disagree; it seemed to me that such exclamations are typical of Steve's and my style. However, I realized after consideration that what made it different was the fact that we were uttering these exclamations against the background of silence. In a conversation in which one of us is telling a story, such exclamations ordinarily come as overlaps or at least rapidly paced in the interchange, where they have the effect of greasing the conversational wheels by encouraging the narrative teller. In fact, I suddenly wondered why these long pauses occurred in the midst of the narrative.

It was only after another pause of a second that Chad continued the story, rather hesitantly:

(28)   Chad: Or whether it was léarned behavior, or was w whether

it was ... uh <u>learned</u> behavior, o:r genetic, or

hormonal or what. /?as they were gonna/

David explained that he and Chad interrupted their story and paused because of my reaction (23) 'WHAT!' My sudden, loud, and high-pitched exclamation stopped them because its marked paralinguistic features were unexpected. David and Chad wondered what was wrong, what my outburst could mean, and they waited to find out. This, then, created a pause that was completely unexpected and unexplained for Steve and me, so we filled it with exclamations (liking nothing less than silence in a busy conversation). Only after ascertaining that I was not going to follow up my shriek with anything else did Chad continue what he began in (24), still hesitant as a result of his uncertainty about the significance of my extreme reaction.

David's insightful observation about this dynamic was proven correct, when the same phenomenon occurred while I was talking to Chad during playback. We were listening to the taped segment about Goffman, which has been referred to earlier. On the tape, Chad offered some observations about Goffman for the first time. Shutting off the tape recorder, Chad commented that he felt free to do this at the time because he was addressing himself to Peter, not me, and Peter did not know anything about the subject. This insight was so helpful and interesting to me that I showed my appreciation by exclaiming, 'Oh:: How interesting!' My exclamation 'Oh::' was sudden and drawn out, and I said, 'How interesting' in a voice that showed intensity through exaggerated low pitch and thick quality. As soon as I said this, Chad stopped short, and there was a fleeting look of astonishment on his face. I immediately tried to repair the situation by repeating, 'That's interesting', in a more matter-of-fact way: faster, more clipped, with higher pitch. Suddenly I recalled David's exegesis of the effect of my extreme reaction to their story about the gay voice. I asked Chad if my extreme response had stopped him just then. He admitted that it had.

This experience also demonstrates how awareness of stylistic differences can operate. I could not help responding to Chad in a way that I 'knew' would make him uncomfortable because my response was automatic. However, once the utterance was out, and I saw his reaction, I could catch what had happened and comment on it. Thus we could understand our reactions to each other's styles, although we could not change them.

During playback, David pointed out yet another instance of pragmatic synonymy. This one contrasts expressive as opposed to understated evaluation. (*Evaluation* in this sense, following Labov 1972, is a speaker's way of showing her/his attitude toward what s/he is saying.) He noted that Chad's (28) and Steve's (29) were synonymous, although on the surface they could not have been more different:

(28)   Chad: Or whether it was léarned behavior, or was w whether

                it was ... uh <u>learn</u>ed behavior, o:r genetic, or

                hormonal or what. ⌐ /? as they were gonna/

(29)   Steve: ⌊ Ooo that makes my skín creep. .... ew:
                                      p,dec

Chad's (28) seemed to me to be a straightforward (if somewhat discursive) statement, without judgment on the part of the speaker. Yet David pointed out that Chad's running together a list of alternatives in a monotonous tone, ending with something hedgy and mumbled like 'or what', is his way of belittling what he is talking about, of showing that the ideas he is reporting are repugnant, and he wishes to dissociate himself from them. Steve's (29), with its slowed pace, deliberate emphasis, exaggerated and metaphoric statement of his reaction, and 'revulsion sound' (Goffman 1981) ('ew:'), is HIS way of dissociating himself from the subject because he finds it repugnant. Steve uses marked intonation and voice quality to show disgust; Chad uses extra words and monotonous tone. Chad's is a style of nuance and understatement, Steve's of expressiveness and overstatement.

A similar contrast can be seen in the discussion that immediately follows the one about the gay voice. It is the discussion of adoption that is sparked by Peter's summary of the article he read reporting research showing that the IQ's of adopted children are more closely correlated with those of their natural parents than those of their adoptive parents. As soon as Peter finishes his observation, Steve exclaims, 'Oh, I believe that!' and I say, 'Oh, of course', and laugh. Steve's exclamation is timed to immediately follow Peter's comment with no pause, and mine immediately follows Steve's at an equally fast pace. Steve's comment is loud and mine is high-pitched. Once more it is interesting to see that we operate as a team; if our strategies are similar to start with, the response of one seems to trigger that of the other.

Following Steve's and my loud responses, David and Chad agree with us with the muted responses 'uhuh' and 'mhm', respectively. During playback, Chad said that he did not react so swiftly and openly to Peter's remarks because he did not know how the rest of us felt about that sort of argument (i.e. heredity vs. environment). Chad was assuring rapport by avoiding disagreement.

In listening to this segment of the tape, I felt that it was rude of Steve and me to react so precipitously to Peter's observation and reject it out-of-hand. I felt that I would not have done so on my own; not that I would not have felt that the results of the study were obvious, but I would not have said so in such a peremptory way, had I not been echoing Steve. I expected Peter, during playback, to report that he felt hurt. Quite the contrary, Peter remarked, on hearing this segment, that the precipitous response, dismissing his comments as obvious, was a verbal device he himself uses. He said, 'It was the sort of thing that drove [my former wife] crazy about living with me. She would consider that a put-down, whereas I expect people to say, "Well look! It really is interesting."' Thus Peter verbalized one aspect of the high-involvement strategy that has been discussed: the expectation that, having something to say, speakers will say it. It is not the burden of the interlocutor to make it comfortable and convenient for others to express their ideas, but rather to be free and spontaneous with reactions. In answer to my direct question of whether Steve's response sounded like a put-down at Thanksgiving, Peter said no: 'It sounds like Steve'. Then he added, with some satisfaction, that the conversation continued on his topic for some time, so clearly people had been interested, and, there-fore, his contribution had been well received.

Getting to the Point

As has already been noted and as Peter himself observed, the IQ topic sparked a story round about adopted children. Steve told two stories about adopted children he knew, I told one, and David told one. David's story cohered thematically and contributed to the round, but there is evidence that Steve felt David did not get to the point in a way he expected.

Let us compare Steve's and David's adoption stories and the reac-tions they triggered from listeners. Here is Steve's first story:

(1) Steve: In fact òne of my stúdents told me for the first time,

I taught her for over a yéar. .... That she was

adópted, and then I thought .. -uh- ... <u>that</u> explains
            p   *acc*

.. <u>so</u> many things.

(2) Deborah: What.⌐That she was →

(3) Steve: └Cause she's só: dífferent⌐from her móther

    Deborah: └smárter than she

should have been? or stùpider →

⌐than she should've been. [*chuckle*]

(4) Steve: └It wasn't smárt or stùpid, àctually, it was just she

was <u>so</u> different. ...... Just '<u>different</u>.
         Deborah: hm ⌐

In response to Steve's story, I express doubt of his premise; I re-mark, 'But you often find kids that are quite different from their par-ents, don't you?' and Sally supports my objection: 'That's seems very unusual that that that the kid didn't pick up his his unnatural par-ents' .... characteristics'. To prove his point, Steve tells another story, about a woman that he and Sally had both known:

Deborah: ⌐the ... sort of

(5)   Steve: Remember what Barbara Thompson? Barbi Thompson told us?

(6)   Sally: What.

(7)   Steve: That she met a half sister? ⌐/?   ?   / → ⌐
                                         Peter: ⌐/? This article?/ ⌐

When they were thírty years old? .... that .. she had

néver met before? It was a hálf sister? It was her

fáther's ˌchìld. ..... And they had all the same

mánnerisms.

[*general exclamations*]

(8) Deborah: But they could have gotten the mannerisms from the
                                                           f⌐

(9)   Steve: ⌐No. The father didn't líve with the other kid. Or

didn't live with Barbi. ... I don't remember.⌐

(10) Deborah: ⌐You're

right. That's <u>very weird</u>.

(11)   Steve: So::
               [*creaky voice*]

                    ....

David then told a story that supports Steve's point:

(12)   David: My u:m ... my aúnt's two kids are adopted, and they
               were both adopted from different .... famili- different
               móthers.

(13)   Steve: Yeah. And?⌐

(14)   David: ⌐And they're just 'dífferent from each other
               and dìfferent from anyone in my fámily. .... They're
                                                    Steve: hm

               not like each óther at àll.

The effects and rhythm of Steve's story, (1)–(4), and David's,
(12)–(14), were quite different. For one thing, the focus of Steve's
narrative is his own personal reaction to the information that his student
was adopted. That is, while the point of the story is to demonstrate the
fact that adopted children are more like their biological parents than
their adoptive parents, Steve dramatizes this point by recreating his

emotional experience. In contrast, David tells about his aunt's two children without saying anything about his participation or how he feels about it. For Steve, the personal involvement between himself and his subject matter is paramount. In contrast, David tells about the content, not his personal involvement in it.

It is highly likely that this difference—i.e. Steve's expectation that a story will be about the speaker's feelings about what s/he is saying— contributes to Steve's dissatisfaction when David tells his story. Steve's prompt (13) 'Yeah. And?' is clearly impatient. Examining Steve's story, I noticed that I prompt Steve during his telling. But the nature of the prompting and the effect of the story-plus-prompts are quite different.

Steve's story is told in a series of alternate up-turned and down-turned clauses. His opening statement (1) 'One of my students told me for the first time', ends with rising intonation. The next clause, 'I taught her for over a year', is spoken quickly, with rather low pitch, ending abruptly with falling intonation. The intonation and pace mark it as a parenthetical remark within the surrounding sentence, 'One of my students told me for the first time that she was adopted'. The continuation of that sentence, 'that she was adopted', also ends with phrase-final intonation (i.e. more to come), while the final sentence in the contribution (1) 'that explains .. so many things', is spoken quickly and abruptly, with marked falling intonation. This rising clause, falling clause contour carries the reader rhythmically through the narrative. At the end of (1), there is a marked sense of finality. I believe this explains why I chose that moment to offer (2) 'What. That she was smarter than she should have been, or stupider than she should've been'. This question feeds Steve his next line. It does not show lack of understanding of the point of his story, nor impatience with him for his pacing. In fact, Steve does not wait for me to finish my question (2) but goes right into his explanation (3), which overlaps with my question (2). For my part, I go right on with my question even at the same time that he is answering it, and Steve incorporates my question into his continuation/response (4). Thus Steve and I overlap during a considerable portion of his story, and there are no pauses between question-answer components, but rather they weave into each other to make an inextricably intertwined story/response entity.

There is a similar rhythmic pattern in Steve's second story, (5)–(11). Again, there is dramatic shifting from high pitch and rising intonation on three clauses (shown in the transcription by question marks) followed by marked falling intonation ending on very low pitch on the fourth clause, 'It was her father's child'. At that point there is a long pause (1.5 seconds) before Steve delivers the climax in a fast and deliberately matter-of-fact sounding coup: 'And they had all the same mannerisms'. The pauses in Steve's narrative are all functional.[1] The first pause, after 'thirty years old', could not be seen as relinquishing the floor because of the sharp rising intonation on the preceding phrase. The pause just before the final sentence in (7) follows the rapidly spoken clauses and, therefore, seems deliberate, not hesitant.

When David begins his story, (12), he begins, as he did his earlier story, with a number of cues that show hesitance about what he is about to say. First there is a false start ('my'), then a filler ('u:m'), then a half-second pause. Within the story, he pauses after 'different' and then has another false start: 'famili- different mothers'. It is then that Steve asks (13) 'Yeah. And?' Thus, it seems likely that Steve's impatience is also sparked by the fact that David's pauses, unlike Steve's, are seemingly random rather than dramatic devices. In this sense, Steve's prompt is designed to help David along, rather like saying, 'Okay, don't worry about background. I'm with you. Now get to the point'. In contrast, my prompts to Steve during his story asked him to elaborate upon a point he had already made, not to get to the point.

If Steve's prompt, (13), indicates dissatisfaction with the way David is telling a story, the dissatisfaction works both ways. In another segment, it is clear that Steve does not tell a story the way David expects. At the very beginning of the taped conversation, there has been much overlapping talk and parallel discussions. At one end of the table, Steve has been showing David pictures of his little niece (Peter's child), and he has commented that 'she looks like a little girl already'. There is some intervening talk. Peter, Sally, and I have been discussing cowboy boots. Steve suddenly switches to our conversation and his voice prevails over the entire group:

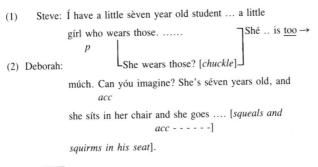

(1)   Steve: Í have a little sèven year old student ... a little

       girl who wears those. ...... ⌉Shé .. is <u>too</u> →

           p ⌊

(2)   Deborah: ⌊She wears those? [*chuckle*]⌋

       múch. Can yóu imagine? She's séven years old, and

         acc

       she síts in her chair and she goes .... [*squeals and*

           acc - - - - - -]

     squirms in his seat].

---

[1]To say they are functional does not imply that they are consciously calculated.

(3) Deborah: Oh: Go:d. … She's only SEVen?

(4)   Steve: And I say well .. hów about let's do sò-and-so. And

                                                                    acc

she says … ⸢Okay. … ⸢Jùst like that.
- - - - -]   [*squealing*]

(5) Deborah: ⸢Oh:::

              ⌊ *p*

(6)   David: ⌊What does it méan.
                p,acc

(7)   Steve: It's just so … ⸢she's acting like such a little gírl already.

                              p

In telling about his student (1)–(4), Steve does not actually state his point at all. Rather, he illustrates it by mimicking the child's mannerisms and speech style. My quick response is (3) to use the characteristic strategy of repeating back an element of Steve's story in echo/mock disbelief: 'She's only SEVen?' (I also did this in (2) 'She wears those'?) My response (3) is expressive through exaggerated intonation and amplitude. When Steve finishes his story (4), David and I respond simultaneously: I groan in commiseration (5) but David asks (6) 'What does it mean?' Steve's explanation (7) is a repetition, in almost the same words and in precisely the same syntactic paradigm with the same intonational pattern as he had used just before, when showing David pictures of his niece:

> Earlier: She looks like a little .. girl already.
>
> now (7): She's acting like such a little girl already.

Steve made this earlier remark to David; I was engaged at the time in the parallel conversation with Peter and Sally about boots. So David should have been more likely to understand Steve's illustration of the same phenomenon in the story about his student. For me, the point of Steve's story represents a change in focus; the connection to the subject of boots is only superficial.[2] Nonetheless it is David who misses the point of the story.

During playback, David said he still felt that Steve had not really told the point of his story. I got the impression that David had not so

---

[2]Such a superficial coherence is acceptable to introduce a story because this is not a round. It seems that within this system, just as personal statements have a certain priority, so do stories. Once a round has begun, however, cohesion is more strictly constrained.

much been unable to understand Steve's point as he was annoyed that Steve had not really made it; that is, Steve had not told the story right. David noted that even after he asked Steve 'What does it mean?' Steve's explanation, (7) 'She's acting like such a little girl already', did not explain what he was trying to say about her. David noted that 'such a little girl' to him meant 'just like a person', or 'grown up', as opposed to 'like an infant'. What Steve meant and should have said was that she was acting like a 'coquette.' David continued that it made him uncomfortable for Steve to squeal and squirm in his seat, imitating the girl's manner. This acting out of the story seemed to him a breach of good taste.

In listening to this segment, Chad noted that David's question (6) 'What does it mean' was making overt what he himself might have wondered. That is, although he guessed that Steve meant that the girl was acting too coquettish, he would have wanted that made clear. I then asked, given that he had a pretty good idea of what Steve meant, why would he ask in a way that showed no comprehension at all? Chad replied that that way he would not risk making himself look foolish, in case he had gotten the wrong idea. Once again, in Chad's and David's system, it is better to refrain from committing oneself, lest one be wrong; in mine, it is better to make a try, because the rapport value of having understood correctly is potentially more important than the possible negative value of having been wrong.

There is probably another level of interaction that contributes to the swiftness with which I participated in Steve's story and the distance that David felt. The point of Steve's story was expected to me. It is the kind of observation that I might make myself, that I have made numerous times. It is the sort of observation that Steve and I often say to each other in conversation, based on our mutually and repeatedly reinforced attitudes toward sex roles. In this way, shared strategies extend to expectations about what will be said, and what can be assumed about others' attitudes, in the spirit of Mills' (1940) notion of *vocabularies of motive*. For Steve and me, it is obvious that it is undesirable for little girls to act stereotypically feminine, and we expect each other to tell stories with this as their point.

Steve's strategy in demonstrating rather than describing his student's manner is similar to the one he uses in the earlier example about the student who was adopted. When he says, in that story, 'and then I thought -uh-', Steve does not explain that he thought, 'This child is so different from her parents.' Rather, he dramatized his own reaction by demonstrating his surprise through a grunt bounded by a pair of glottal stops.

Meaning in Intonation

It is part of Steve's style to tell a story the point of which is in the intonation rather than the verbal content. This can be seen strikingly in the following example. I have commented on how attractive the table is; Steve has laid out whole walnuts and tangerines still attached to stems and leaves. A humorous discussion followed about 'making things pretty', in which David suggested that the reason Steve likes to make things pretty is that he's gay. Peter then said that he also likes to make things pretty, and he's not gay. Amid general laughter, Steve said to Peter, 'But do you make things as pretty as I make them?' He said this in a mock-taunting tone, like a boy razzing his brother. Peter picked up Steve's game and responded in kind, saying 'Prettier', also in mock-taunting tone, so that the two of them seemed to be figuratively sticking their tongues out at each other. Everyone laughed at the joke, there was a brief pause, and then Steve told this story:

(1)   Steve: Línda said to me ..... Can I have that can Í have
                that pen to play with? .... And I said⌐
(2) Deborah: ⌐That pén to
                play with?
(3)   Steve: I was playing .. with a pén. She said. Can Í have that
                p,acc
                pen to play with? .... I said Nó, take thís pen. She
                said Nó I want that pen. And I said ... I'm playing
                with this pen. ... She said ... Wé coulda just been
                                            acc

                foúr years old.

Steve tells this story as an illustration of another incident in which he engaged in mock-childlike fighting, just as he and Peter just did. The cohesion between the two incidents is in the intonation used by him and Peter in the one case and by him and Linda in the other. He never states that point; it resides in the intonation pattern and the juxtaposition of the stories. As Steve tells the story about his earlier conversation with

Linda, he recreates the tone and voice quality with which they spoke, in the same way that he mimicked his little student in the other story. Moreover, he begins the story with no orientation (Labov 1972), i.e. introduction or contextualization. He simply leaps into the narrative events.

As usual I respond after Steve's very first sentence. In this case, I question the context, because he has jumped into the story without explanation, so the thematic cohesion, which resides in the intonation, has not yet become apparent. He begins (1) 'Linda said to me', quite as if he had already been talking about Linda. Therefore, I ask (2) 'That pen to play with?' Using only intonation as a cue, I repeat his phrase to ask, 'What are you talking about?' My question barely slows Steve at all. He explains quickly, with low amplitude (3), 'I was playing with a pen'. The way he dismisses this explanation, which is a minimal explanation, of the context indicates that this is not where the significance of the story lies, so it is not necessary to spend much time talking about it. Steve then returns to his story, with hardly a hitch in timing at all. He backs up and begins again from the beginning: (3) 'She said, "Can I have that pen to play?"' Because his story depends for its impact on the intonational pattern of the interchange between him and Linda, it is necessary for him to give the entire sequence without interruption, starting from Linda's first request for 'that pen to play with' up to the intonation climax, (3) 'Wé coulda just been foúr years old', which is spoken very fast, with very abrupt falling intonation.

The strategy of backing up and starting from the beginning to preserve an intonational pattern is the same that Steve used in the earlier example of the Coliseum discussion. There Steve began, 'Here's Columbus Circle, here's Central Park West', but was interrupted by Peter and me suggesting (erroneously) that the building he had in mind was the Huntington Hartford museum. Steve then said 'Nuhnuhno', quickly dismissing our error (much as in the present example he dispensed with my question about the context of the 'pen to play with') and then began again with the same intonational pattern: 'Here's Central Park West, here's Broadway'. The fact that the words have changed a bit—that is, 'Central Park West' and 'Broadway' have replaced 'Columbus Circle' and 'Central Park West', respectively—does not change the rhythm of the sentence. The intonation pattern remains just the same, and this is what gives the talk its shape.

In addition, it is interesting that Steve uses the same rhythmic pattern to signal the climax of this story as he used in the story about his student who was adopted.

Adopted student example (1): and then I thought .. -uh- ... thát explains só many
                                                  things.

Present example (3): She said ... Wé coulda just been foúr years old.

After Steve tells the story about Linda and the pen, there is general laughter. Then Peter says to David, 'You missed it', and David says, 'Yes I did'. Listening to the story on tape, David commented that he could easily see the point of Steve's story, but he thought it fell flat. Again, the problem seems to be not his inability to follow such logic, but his sense that this is not how a story should be told.

Cooperative vs. Impatient Prompting

I wondered about the difference between prompting someone in a cooperative way and dragging a story out of them. The contrast between these two prompting phenomena emerges in a comparison of stories told by Peter and Sally, and how I react to them.

Cooperative prompting questions can be seen in the following story. Peter has just commented that he wonders how his children's view of life is affected, now that he is having relationships with new women. As he is talking, the entire group is listening and reacting, but it is I who actually prompt him in the storytelling:

(1)   Peter: I mean .... y'know Jonny, ... waking up each morning

                 with some .. new .. lády in the house. [*others laugh*]
                                                        [*laughing*]

                 ...... 'Did YOU stay overníght last night? WHERE did
                                                      acc

                 YOU SLEEP'. [*laughter*] .... ₁I slept in your
                 Deborah:ˡ Yeahˡ [*laughing*]

                 daddy's bed'. ... 'Whère did my ' Daddy sleep'. [*laughter*]
                                                  f

                                      ....

(2) Deborah: What'd she say.

A little further on in the same talk, I prompt Peter again:

(3)   Peter: The other day he said ... 'Why were you guys making só
                                                            [*laughing*]

                 much nóise?' [*laughter*]

.....

(4) Deborah: Díd he rèally? .... And what'd you s͡ay:.

At first my questions seem similar to my questions of David when he was telling about his friend's experience at a meeting at which 'the gay voice' was discussed. However, on close inspection, the instances of questions are really quite different. My questions of David are trying to get him to be specific about what he has thus far only hinted at. That is, in that interchange, David suggests that what his friend Randy heard people saying at the meeting was somehow related to what I have mentioned about women's language, but he has not said what the connection was. Therefore, I ask, 'So what was he saying?' then 'What were they doing?' and again, 'What was he saying?' All this time, I have the feeling that I have not been told what the point of David's story is, and I should have been told.

In the present interchange, Peter has begun and stopped his story too, but he seems to have stopped on purpose, for effect. The loud laughter of the group confirms that his point has been appreciated. When I ask Peter (2) 'What'd she say?' I am prompting him to continue, to tell the next line. My question comes after a long pause of four seconds, filled with general laughter. This is the same thing that is going on in (4), when I follow a high-pitched exclamation, 'Did he really?' with the prompt, 'And what'd you say?' My tone shows appreciation of the significance of the moment Peter has described. 'Did he really' is spoken with exaggerated intonation to show that Peter's story has had an effect, and the last word, 'say', in 'And what'd you say' is drawn out and spoken in an exaggerated intonation contour that shifts from high to low pitch. Thus the question serves both as a prompt and a show of interest in the story as it has proceeded thus far. (In the terms of conversational analysts, the question is what Yngve 1970 calls a backchannel response.)

In telling this story, Peter uses intonation and tone to frame direct quotations. He does not introduce reported speech by saying, 'He said' or 'She said'. Rather, he mimics his son's and his girlfriend's speech. The fact that he is quoting is communicated by the tone, intonation, and voice quality.

Throughout the Thanksgiving dinner conversation, Sally has a hard time getting herself heard. She speaks in a soft voice with high pitch and lots of pauses within her speech. According to her own report, she generally waits for silence before saying something, and she does not find many moments of silence in this fast-paced conversation. Sally has had much experience with conversations of this sort; she lived with Steve for six years. But conversational control habits are learned early (Anderson 1977; Schieffelin 1979) and are automatic; once they have solidified, continued exposure does not necessarily result in learning a new system. It may merely intensify one's feelings of inability to understand that system, or rather one's feelings about the people who behave in a way that has different meaning in one's own system. This explains the research finding (Vassiliou, Triandis, Vassiliou, and McGuire 1972) that increased exposure to members of different groups often leads to increased rather than decreased negative stereotyping.

When Sally does find a place to interject her speech into the conversation, her troubles are not over. It is consistently difficult for her to pursue a topic until her complete thought is out, and it is difficult for Peter and me to figure out what her main point is. For example, note the following interchange in which Sally tells what she ate on the plane from Canada to California that day:

....

(1)   Sally: Oh I was amàzed to see the uh ... the méal on the
               aírplane today.

(2)   Peter: What was it?

(3)   Sally: It was ... a bágel with crèam chèese .....

(4)   David: ⌐What's this?

(5)   Peter: ⌐For lunch?

(6)   Sally: At ‚lunch, ... a bagel with cream ⌐ cheese

(7)   Peter: ⌐ That's .. that's
Air Canada, right? ... um Pacific⌐

(8) Deborah: ⌐A .. a bagel
       ⌐and créam cheese?

(9)   Sally: ⌐It was United.   A bagel and cream cheese, ...
                            acc
and a whole pile of <u>ham</u>.
[laughter]

Sally begins her story at a point in the conversation when there is a brief pause. So far so good. She begins by stating the background for what she wants to say (1), much as David began his story about his friend Randy. Sally's opening also is characterized by a pause, and the filler 'uh' plus repetition of the determiner 'the' give her contribution a hesitant quality.

Peter gives Sally encouragement when he asks (2) 'What was it.' This seems to be cooperative prompting. Sally then continues with (3) 'It was ... a bagel with cream cheese.' This statement ends with steady intonation and a pause. Peter then asks (5) 'For lunch?' It is clear from the tape, and Peter stated so during playback, that he had the impression that Sally had finished her story. Indeed most informants who listened to this segment made this interpretation. Because Sally stopped after 'cream cheese', and her intonation did not rise, Peter assumed that her complete story was that she had been served a bagel and cream cheese on the plane. But after Sally answers Peter's question with (6) 'At lunch', she backs up to repeat 'a bagel with cream cheese'. Again Peter asks a question (7) about which airline she was on. I interrupt Peter (who has interrupted Sally) to respond to her story by repeating what I, like Peter, think is her already uttered main point. Yet again, Sally answers Peter's question with (9) 'It was United' and then once more backs up and repeats, 'a bagel and cream cheese',[3] but this time she says it quickly, with a sense of urgency, and pauses for only half a second before adding what has been the point of her story all along— that the bagel and cream cheese were served with 'a whole pile of ham'. The ham is ironic because bagel and cream cheese are typical Jewish food, while ham is nonkosher and typically non-Jewish. The fact that this is a more significant point is attested to by the loud laughter that follows Sally's mention of the ham. Steve exclaims, 'That's disgusting', in mock-disgust.

During playback, Sally said she could not understand why Peter kept interrupting her story to question her about irrelevant details. In other words, Peter's and my prompts seemed obstructive to her. The reason for them was that Peter and I had not understood the point of her story—indeed, missed the fact that she had not gotten to the point yet— and were trying to show interest in what seemed like a rather pointless story.

Peter and I did not expect Sally to pause before making her main point, without indicating through intonation that more was to come. For

---

[3] It's interesting to note that Sally says 'a bagel WITH cream cheese', her first two utterances, but I say 'a bagel AND cream cheese'. For me this is formulaic. When Sally ratifies my echo of her utterance in (10), she switches to AND. This is apparently the effect of the echo. There are numerous examples in the conversation of people repeating things that they would not ordinarily say, because the person they are echoing said them that way.

Sally, the pause is necessary. In (9), she succeeds in communicating the fact that more is to come by rushing through 'a bagel and cream cheese' very rapidly with a breathy quality, but she still pauses before adding 'and a whole pile of ham'.

A similar situation arises when Sally tells of another experience later in the conversation. The talk has focused on hands. Steve had commented that short, stubby hands are better for playing the piano. Sally says,

(1) Sally: Í shook hánds with ‚Rúbinstein once? ....⌈And his hand

(2) Steve: ⌊Yeàh we díd

        togéther.

(3) Sally: ⌈That's ríght. ⌈We were togéther. ⌈Wasn't it incrédible?

(4) Steve: Oh it was like a cushion.⌉
        [*laughing*]

(5) David: ⌊What's this?

(6) Sally: I ... we shook we shook hànds with Rúbinstein.

(7) Steve: ⌊Rúbinstein's hànds.⌟

        ......

(8) Deborah: And he had?⌉ →

(9) Sally: ⌊His hands⌉ .... →

     Deborah: ⌊Short stubby hands?

Just as Steve was earlier seen to impatiently prompt David to get to the point of a story by saying, 'Yeah. And?' here I ask Sally (8) 'And he had? Short stubby hands?' My feeling as I listen to this on the tape now coincides with what I appear to have felt then, that because Sally brought up the fact that she shook hands with Rubinstein she should have continued to tell what it was about his hand that was remarkable. The two-second pause after (7) is enough to indicate to me that Sally does not intend to say more. Steve had just been saying that short stubby hands are good for playing the piano, so I supply this as a plausible point for Sally's contribution. (It is typical of my style to supply a point if someone else does not provide one when I expect them to.) In fact, that is not what Sally had in mind. Although Steve had talked about short stubby fingers, Sally had commented, 'and you need thick pads on the end.' However, she said this in such a low voice that it was almost inaudible and it was not picked up on. Steve quickly stated the point in

(4), 'Oh it was like a cushion,' but I apparently was listening for the point from Sally, not Steve.

The conversation continued this way:

(8) Deborah: And he had? →
(9)　　Sally:　　　　　⌐His hands⌐ .... →
　　Deborah:　　　　　　　　⌐Short stubby hands?⌐
　　Sally:　　　　　　　　　　　　　⌐They were

like ... jélly. They were like .... they were like ...
Steve: ⌐a famous concert pianist.⌐

pútty. ... Just .. complétely sóft →
Deborah: ⌐Really?⌐

and　　⌐límp. .... Just músh. It was as though there
Steve: ⌐mush [Deborah *chuckles*]

was　ńo bóne.　⌐
Steve: ⌐and warm.⌐

(10) Deborah: And short stubby fingers?
(11)　　Sally: ⌐Short stubby fingers but just ... tótally cóvered
acc- - - - - - - - - - - - - -]

with ....

(12)　Steve:　fat⌐
(13)　Sally:　　⌐fat.

Here again is Sally's characteristic strategy of pausing before uttering the crucial word, as she did in (9) with 'jelly' and 'putty'.

(9) They were like ... jélly. They were like .... they were like ... pútty.

In (10) and (11) Sally and I almost exactly replicate the devices we both used in the bagels interchange. When I ask (10) 'And short stubby fingers?' I am supplying, with question intonation, the point of Sally's story. She lets me know that this is fact but not the point by repeating what I have said quickly and with low pitch, and then proceeding to the real point, which she utters after a pause, and with some help from Steve: that Rubinstein's fingers were 'covered with fat.' In the bagels example, I repeated, with question intonation, 'A bagel and cream cheese?' and Sally repeated these words quickly then continued, after a pause, 'and a whole pile of ham'.

The fact that Sally pauses before saying the key word often leads some others of us to conclude that she is done. When it is clear that she is not done, her pause sometimes tempts Steve to supply her with the word, perhaps as if the pause is evidence that she is having trouble finding the right word, and he wants to help her out. Perhaps, too, he is simply showing that he knows where her talk is headed. In answer to my questioning during playback, Sally said that she does not mind that kind of help; it makes her feel protected and cared for. Certainly Steve offers it in a cooperative spirit. It is clear, however, that many people do not like that kind of help, as evidenced by such familiar comments as 'Don't tell me what I'm going to say', or, 'Don't put words in my mouth'. The writer of the *New West* article, for example, begins by stating that he is a slow talker, and he complains, 'But my deliberate gait results in . . . problems: All my life, for instance, people have been finishing my sentences for me' (Esterly 1979, p. 67).

What the Point Can Be

An even more striking discrepancy arises when Sally tells a longer story. The only extended story she tells during the taped conversation, it occurs late in the evening, which may account for the fact that she felt comfortable enough to offer a story. A flyer advertising a concert series featuring Sally's group is lying on the table, because Sally had brought it out earlier in the evening in connection with a discussion of cartoons. The flyer is illustrated with cartoons (see Figures 1a, b, c, & d). At this point in the conversation, I notice the flyer and ask Sally whether she did the lettering. She answers that she did and adds that the illustrations were 'done' by Howard Pyle (a long deceased cartoonist). Chad makes a comment about the cartoons, and Sally then continues:

(1)   Sally: <u>Yeah</u>. .... Yeah. .... It's a wònderful póem that goes
                  f

            with the .. with the .. píctures. ...The: ... the

            ... rich lády, ... uh ... takes in the píg? And makes

            him her fríend? And decides that she's going to make

            him into a géntleman. .... So he becomes a géntleman
                                    acc ------------------------]

            and falls in love with a .. falls in love with a lády.

            .... And ... and then he he proposes to the lády, and

all he can say is .. ⌜whee-whee-. [*chuckles*] .....

And that's

      ...

(2) Deborah: Whó turns him into a pìg?

(3)   Chad: No. He ís a pig.⌉

(4)   Sally: ⌊He ís a pig. ⌝

(5) Deborah: ⌊He ís a pig.⌉

                Chad: ⌊Right.

(6)   Sally: And the rich lady ... decides to bring him up, ... to

          be a géntleman.

(7) Deborah: And he acts like a géntleman, except he ... loóks

          like a pìg?

          [Sally *laughs*]

(8)   David: ⌐And all he can sáy is

(9)   Sally: ⌊And he learns he learns .... he learns to dance, and

          and and have the elegant .... the gráces, ... of the

          elegant mán, ... ⌐but

(10) Deborah: ⌊And hòw does it eńd.

(11)   Sally: He proposes to the lády? And all he can sáy, ... when

          he opens his móuth is ⌜whee- whee-.

(12) Deborah: [*chuckle*] And thén?⌉→

(13)   Sally: ⌊And thén⌉

    Deborah: ⌊Does she accépt him?

(14)   Sally: No:. Loók. Loók at the last pícture.

          f

          ....

(15) Deborah: What. She's .. looks uh she .. scówls at him?

(16)   Sally: Yes.

(17) Deborah: She says is thís the thanks I get?

(18)   Sally: [*laughs*]

It is clear from my questions and remarks (2), (7), (10), (12), (15), and (17) that I do not understand the point of the story. My question (2) 'Who turns him into a pig?' shows a lack of attention; if I listen to Sally's story on the tape, I easily see that the character began as a pig.

1a

But my other questions reflect a sense of bafflement that I experience anew each time I listen to the story. To Sally, however, the point of the story is obvious. When I ask her (10) 'How does it end?' she merely repeats (11) what she already said in (1): 'He proposes to the lady? And all he can say when he opens his mouth is whee-whee'. By way of

1b

1c

'explanation', she adds the phrase 'when he opens his mouth'. To Sally, this is the end; the fact that a lady would not marry a pig who cannot talk is self-evident. This is similar to what happened in the earlier example in which Steve told about his student, the little girl. When David asked what he meant to point out, Steve responded by repeating something he had said previously which to him seemed transparent but to David was begging the question: 'She's such a little girl already' (p. 114).

During playback, Sally averred that my responses were most disconcerting to her. It seemed as if I was not paying any attention at all. Her annoyance can be seen in her reaction to my questions and comment at the time. When I ask (12) 'And then? Does she accept him?' the

1d

way Sally says (14) 'No:' is most strident for her: her voice is much louder than usual, and she draws out the vowel. She then says, 'Look. Look at the last picture'. She clearly feels that if I only pay attention, I'll get the point. I do in fact look at the picture and describe what I see (15), 'She scowls at him,' but I still do not get the point. From my perspective, if I am to suspend realistic judgment to accept that a pig learned to dance, why should he not also learn to talk? And if a lady would raise a pig in her house and dance with him, why not marry him too? The very long pause of 5 seconds following (14) attests to my confusion.

My question (17) 'She says is this the thanks I get?' is my characteristic attempt to supply an explanation when I feel no satisfactory one has been offered. It reveals yet another misunderstanding of Sally's story. I am under the impression that the lady who raised the pig and the lady he proposed to are one and the same. I have gotten this impression from Sally's intonation in telling the story. When she says, in (1) 'the rich lády, uh, takes in the píg', and when she later says that the pig 'falls in love with a lády', the emphasis is on 'lady' in both cases, in the same way. I would have expected her to differentiate by saying, 'He falls in love with another lady'. In rapid speech, 'with the lady' and 'with a lady' are indistinguishable. From Sally's point of view, however, my question was very odd because she assumes I have understood that there are two different ladies as can be seen in the cartoon. But rather than confront me directly, she responded by laughing (18) and letting the matter drop.

In this case, there are clearly cultural differences causing problems. In playback, Sally explained that the obvious meaning of the story is allegorical: the pig represents the bourgeoisie, and the point is that no matter how much you educate and dress them up, their basic nature will not be changed. Neither I nor any other person at the Thanksgiving dinner nor any other American for whom I played the story, was able to glean this meaning from it, nor any other meaning either. By contrast, another native British informant who listened to the story said immediately, 'Oh yes, the story shows that you should not get involved with those who are fundamentally different from you'. When I asked if it might have reference to class differences, she said, 'Oh yes of course'. Similarly, but disastrously, I told the story to my hairdresser, who is of working class British background, while he was cutting my hair. Not only was he visibly insulted by the story, but I walked out of his shop with the worst haircut he had ever given me. It seemed that he too had taken the story as an allegory about class differences, reflecting negatively on his class.

In addition to differences in expectations about what stories can be about, there are clearly differences operating about how stories are told. Like Steve in earlier examples, Sally did not overtly state the point of her story; she left it to her audience to draw the conclusions. Her strategy is not to impose, not to insult her audience by hitting them over the head with the point. But her style differs from Steve's in that intonation and direct quotation are not used to dramatize the point either. Sally's style combines the lexical understatement of Steve's with the paralinguistic understatement of Chad's styles.

It is characteristic of our styles, too, that of all those who listened to Sally's story, everyone admitted in playback that they did not get the point, but only I verbalized my confusion with the results that have been seen. Chad, for example, said that he would never risk offending Sally by making it so obvious that he did not see the point. Thus Chad's high-considerateness strategy pays off in rapport, whereas my high-involvement strategy (assuming positive interpersonal relations) causes interpersonal distress. In other words, the feeling of rapport is the result whenever strategies are shared. The use of any strategy with others who do not share its principles and devices can lead to just the opposite of rapport. Ways of telling and responding to stories, then, are an integral part of conversational style.

CHAPTER 6

Irony and Joking

One of the most distinctive aspects of any person's style is the use of humor. Through intonation, pace, voice quality, and nonverbal signals, a speaker can frame an utterance or string of utterances as 'not meant literally'. Such stylized usage can range from sarcasm (in which the intent is not humorous, and often hostile), to irony (which might excite a smile or chuckle), to a joke, in which the main purpose is to entertain. Close examination of the use of irony and joking by members of the Thanksgiving group (there were few instances of sarcasm) contributes further insights into their styles.

Roy (1978) notes in an extended study of irony in conversation that irony vs. nonirony is not a binary distinction but rather a continuum. Clearly, there is some subjectivity involved in classifying utterances as ironic or not ironic, just as there was with classifying utterances as narrative. Roy points out that there are problems with the traditional definitions of irony as 'meaning the opposite of what is said' or 'meaning something different from what is said'. To arrive at a satisfying definition of irony would require a major study in itself. In general, I regarded statements as humorous or ironic if they seemed not to be meant literally and seemed to be intended to amuse.

Roy cites Cutler's (1974) list of intonational cues of irony:

1. nasalization of all or part of an utterance
2. slower rate in all or part
3. exaggerated stress on one or more parts

In many cases these cues were present in utterances I judged ironic, but certainly not in all cases.

Table 2 shows the number of turns and percentages of turns devoted to ironic or humorous statements by members of the Thanksgiving group. The speaker who shows the greatest use of irony and humor is Steve, with 65 or 11 percent of his turns classified as ironic or humorous. In this his use of humor correlates with his use of narrative perhaps contributing to his 'broad' personal style. I am next with 58 humorous or ironic turns, but because my total number of turns is greater than Steve's, the percentage of his turns that were ironic or humorous is greater than mine: 11 percent as opposed to my 7 percent. Interestingly, the person next in line in terms of number of ironic or humorous turns is David. In other words, David and Peter switch places, as Steve and I switch places, in terms of absolute use of irony and humor as opposed to absolute number of contributions. However, the *percentage* of David's turns that are ironic or humorous is 11 percent, which is equal to Steve's percentage. In stark contrast, Chad emerges as the member least given to humor or irony. Although Chad's contributions in absolute number of turns were almost as great as Peter's and greater than David's, his use of irony or humor is much less. In fact, Chad makes only three more ironic or humorous contributions than Sally (10 for Chad, 7 for Sally), and only 2 percent of his turns are devoted to irony or humor, by far the least in the group and far less than David's. Chad's use of humor correlates with his use of narrative, which also accounted for only 2 percent of his turns. This difference may account for the different impressions made

Table 2   Use of Irony and Humor

Name	Number of ironic/humorous turns	Total number of turns	Percentage of turns ironic or humorous
Steve	65	594	11%
Deborah	58	811	7%
David	43	386	11%
Peter	19	417	5%
Chad	10	405	2%
Sally	7	169	4%

by David's and Chad's participation in the group. On hearing the results of the turn count, several members of the group were surprised to learn that Chad had talked as much as he had. We had come away with the impression that he had been very quiet. But in listening to the tape, looking at the transcript, and learning of the turn counts, we realized that Chad had in fact been a very active participant in the conversation. Similarly, we had thought that David had participated more than he had. Sally, for example, when referring to the group as a 'rambunctious crowd', had included David, but not Chad. Yet in number of turns taken, David was less active a participant than Chad, and more talkative only than Sally. It seems likely that the impression that David had participated more than he had, came from the fact that he cracked a lot of jokes (and perhaps that he told long stories). This implies that use of humor makes one's presence felt, at least the kind of humor that David employed (we will see what kind that was, presently).

Peter was next after David, with many fewer turns (19 as opposed to David's 43, my 58, and Steve's 65) and a smaller percentage, as well: 5 percent of Peter's turns were ironic or humorous. Sally is right next to Peter in terms of percentage with 4 percent, but in absolute number of ironic turns, she is at the bottom of the list with 7.

Thus some of the differences in style that characterize the members of the group can be seen in the degree of their use of humor and irony. Even more, the kind of humor that each person employed was distinctive. It seems likely that brand of humor is one of the most highly individualistic aspects of a person's style. Thus, it has been seen that in expectation of conversational control devices such as overlap, rate of speech, use of paralinguistic features, and structuring of narratives, there were many ways in which Chad and David shared expectations, while Steve, Peter and I shared stylistic features. However, in use of humor, Chad and David could not be more different, and Steve, Peter and I also exhibit very different styles.

Steve's most characteristic form of humor is a mocking style by which he exaggerates either his own or someone else's speech patterns. In this sense, his is an irony aimed at style. It is also of the form that Roy (1978:118), following Wayne Booth, calls 'dramatic irony.' By this device, Roy notes, 'the speaker can mean what he says and at the same time disclaim what he says by taking on a role, frequently stereotypical or at least well-defined'. For example, in his role as host, Steve is frequently in the position of giving orders to people and offering them food. He frequently mocks his own behavior in this role by affecting a stereotypical Jewish speech pattern. For example, when someone offers to help him serve, he replies, 'You should sit and relax, dahlink!' His use of the modal 'should', exaggerated intonation, and stylized voice quality and pronunciation are all patterned on the speech of Steve's grandmother, who immigrated to the United States from Poland. Thus he is mocking his own impulse to pattern his hosting behavior on her model. In addition to affecting exaggerated hosting style, Steve stylizes the bossiness that his host role entails. Thus, for example, he says to Sally, who is helping him serve: 'Sally, THAT was for the STUFFing!' His tone affects annoyance far greater than what he might have actually felt, and thereby makes a joke of whatever slight annoyance he actually did feel. This is the attitude that Steve adopts and draws upon with regard to the presence of the tape recorder on the table.

In his role as host, Steve is concerned with making the table attractive. He has placed walnuts and tangerines with green leaves on the table, and he makes a point of taking everything off the table that is not attractive. I placed the tape recorder in the middle of the table with full approval from Steve, but at several times during the occasion, his eyes light upon the machine, and he complains about it in an exaggerated tone.

→(1) Steve: Do ⌐wé have to ⌐hàve this here. ... Does ⌐thís have
to bé here?

(2) Sally: /?/

(3) Deborah: No I mean

(4) Chad: She set it in the middle.

(5) Deborah: G'head. Spóil my dissertàtion. .... I'm gonna put a ⌐ →
→(6) Steve: ⌐Does this have⌐ →

fóotnote.⌐
→Steve: ⌐Does thís have to bé here like thìs.

(7) Chad: It's his.

→(8) Steve: ⌐I mean Marie's.
(9) David: ⌐Well put it on the sálad and then you can do whatever
you wánt with it.

→(10) Steve: Marie':s? I mean, ... just lóok at everything at
this tàble. It's béautiful. And we have to look at
Marié's?

....

(11) Deborah: [*chuckle*]

Each of Steve's statements (1), (6), (8), and (10) is spoken with exaggerated intonation and voice quality showing great annoyance. After complaining about the fact that the tape recorder is spoiling the appearance of the table, he moves on to complain, in the same tone, about the presence of a jar of commercial salad dressing ('Marie's' is the brand name of the dressing that is printed on the jar).

In response to Steve's complaint about the tape recorder, I respond with irony of my own. I affect annoyance at the fact that he is interfering with my dissertation (5). (In fact, I had only the vaguest notion of possibly using the tape recording for my dissertation at that point.) Although I did feel some slight annoyance that Steve was drawing attention to the tape recorder, I did not take his complaint seriously; I did not think he seriously minded it being there; and I did not for a moment consider taking it away. I believed Steve did not mind my taping, and I knew that the only way to tape was to leave the recorder in the middle of the table.

David is responsible for the salad dressing, and his response is quite different from mine. He seems to take Steve's complaint (6) (8) seriously and explains (9) that after the dressing is put on the salad, the bottle can be taken away. 'You can do whatever you want with it', sounds like a genuine expression of annoyance at Steve for complaining.

During playback, David explained his understanding of what was going on. He believed that Steve was truly angry at me for having the tape recorder on the table, and then tried to cover his sincere anger by also saying something about the salad dressing bottle. However, Steve, during his playback session, was speechless at my suggestion that he might have genuinely been angry at me for taping. He liked the idea of my taping, he insisted. He said he truly did not like the tape recorder messing up his table, but he was not thinking clearly about the fact that it had to be there in order to record the conversation. He was just picking up on a fleeting impression he got and exaggerating it for comic effect. He felt the same way about the salad dressing bottle as he did about the recorder.

Steve returns to the mock anger about the tape recorder at two later points in the dinner. One instance has already been discussed in another connection (p. 91). There he says, (10) 'Could we get this off the table?' This first question is said more or less seriously. But Steve immediately moves into his mocking style, making fun of himself by exaggerating his slight annoyance:

(13)   Steve: It keeps coming back on the 'tàble. It must have a will of its ˌòwn.
          That's all I can say.

The third time Steve calls attention to the tape recorder he comments:

(1)   Steve: Be uh have wè been .. ⌐táping? This whole ⌐time?
(2) Deborah: └I'm glad

          I didn't notice it ⌐until just now. [*referring to preceding topic*]
(3)   Chad: └Shè keeps that thing rúnning.

(4)   Steve: I keep I- .. I say, get that thing off the table. She
                                   acc

          says .. oh yeah okay I'll take it off the table and
                   acc

          I look, ... ⏐two minutes later and it's báck.
                                              [*laughter*]

          .... Whàt's to ánalyze. There hasn't been <u>one</u>

          misunderstánding, we've all understood each other <u>perfectly</u>.

(5)   Peter: What do you méan by that.
          [*loud laughter*] ....

(6) Deborah: That's 'two: .... 'Júst forˌgèt about it. 'Só
                                  [*laughter*]

          it's' 'thère. .... [*laughing*] [Steve *laughs*] What

          ˌdo yóu care what I'm gonna dò about it.
          └
(7)   Peter: └I don't mind the táping, I mind the spáce it takes up.

(8) Deborah: It's so unobtrusive.⌐
(9)   Steve: └It's so UGly. ... Éverything on
                                  [Deborah laughs- - - - - - - -

          this table is béautiful except THAT and MarIE's. And
          - - - - - - - - - - - - - - - - - - - [David *chuckles*]

          even Marié's is palatable .. next to THAT. [Deborah *laughs*]

(10)   David: You can éat .. Marié's⌐
(11) Deborah: └It's so sleek,

          [*laughter*] .....

```
                    It's sleek, and black, and and ... ┌ fine,
(12)    Peter:                                          └ You never met

        [name.] Did you?
```

As in the earlier example, I react to Steve's exaggerated annoyance about the presence of the tape recorder by exaggerating my defense of it. Again, Steve's intonation and voice quality indicate extreme annoyance, but it is mock annoyance, and that is why I take it as a joke, laugh, and do not feel it would be appropriate to do anything. Steve does not attempt to make me comply; he simply wants to be able to make a joke about it.

Thus Steve uses the mocking style to exaggerate and laugh at his own speech. At other times, he uses it to affect a speech pattern that is clearly foreign to him. Thus when he is serving wine and I am distracted, he gets my attention by saying, 'Gimme ya glass, baby'. He says this with nasal quality and a clipped, 'tough-guy' manner. My reaction is to laugh and ask, 'Who're you calling baby?' At another time Steve uses a similar style with Peter. In offering tickets to his upcoming concerts, he begins flipping a pack of tickets, then turns to Peter and says, 'How many ya want, Peter'. This is said in the same way as the preceding example, i.e. mock tough style.

A person's stylistic devices change with changing situations and interlocutors. The role of host encourages Steve to use his mocking style as a way of playing that role without taking himself seriously in it. In the last half hour of taped conversation, when dinner is over and everyone is sitting around the table talking, Steve hardly uses these devices at all.

I also occasionally affect exaggerated Jewish style. For example, I say to Steve, 'Si:t, si:t', when he is busy serving food. In this I am building on his humor, as when Steve affected ironic annoyance with regard to my tape recorder, and I responded in kind. Frequently throughout the conversation I make jokes by changing slightly or adding to something that someone else has said. Thus, when I announce that I will tape the conversation, Peter asks, 'Just to see if we say anything interesting?' I answer, 'No. Just to see how you say nothing interesting'. Similarly, in another discussion, Peter is talking about the problem of spending money on children. He comments (ironically):

```
(1)    Peter: Yeah. ... I mean I get -I l I 'líke things .. that you
              p [sighing]
```

can buy with mòney. Y'know it's not like I like to
                [Deborah *laughs*]

súffer and stárve.⌉
[*laughter*]

(2)   Steve: ⌊Peter, you- I think you should

start méditating more. .... [*laughter*] You gòtta

get more into spíritual ⌈things.

(3)   Deborah: ⌊No, maybe he could teach his

kíds to meditate. [*laughter*]

Thus I build on the already established ironic tone by slightly changing Steve's perspective.

At another point, David is telling an extended joke about a fictitious organization he and his friends invented, called NORCLOD (Northern California Lovers of the Deaf). As David embroiders the joke by explaining the rules of the organization, I contribute to his joke by supplying another detail along the lines he established:

(1)   David: u:m ..... and .... um the wáy we were gonna have the

uh the òfficers of the organization the higher up you

go, ... the more héaring people there would be and

then the .. the .. the: cháirperson of the òrganization

was gonna be a héaring person.

(2)   Deborah: That didn't know sígn language.

(3)   David: That didn't .... Yeah. That didn't know sígn language.
                        [*laughter*]

Whereas Steve's irony is mock annoyed, mock tough, or mock solicitous, and dramatized through exaggerated enunciation, Peter's is mock serious. Sally described Peter as 'more sedate' than Steve and me. This impression no doubt comes in part from Peter's serious way of delivering ironic lines, as opposed to Steve's (and David's) dramatized, camping irony. In addition, whereas Steve often follows his ironic comments with laughter (David laughs even more, and I laugh the most and loudest), Peter never laughs after his one-liners, and he often follows them up with genuinely serious statements.

For example, in the example on p. 136, Peter stated (1) 'I like things that you can buy with money. It's not like I like to suffer and starve'. He said this with a serious tone. In the tape-recorder interchange (p. 135), Steve has said, in gross mocking style, (4) 'What's to analyze. There hasn't been <u>one</u> misunderstanding, we've all understood each other <u>perfectly</u>'. (Steve is referring to my early work on the analysis of misunderstandings in conversation.) Peter immediately snaps (5) 'What do you mean by that'. He says this in an utterly serious tone. Its irony comes from the fact that he is pretending to misunderstand, contradicting what Steve has just said. The resultant loud laughter from the group is evidence that his humor is successful, but Peter does not participate in the laughter. Rather, he follows up his joke with a serious statement (7) 'I don't mind the taping, I mind the space it takes up'. (Throughout the dinner, Peter evidences the same preoccupation with getting extraneous things off the table that Steve does.) Steve never makes such a serious statement about the tape recorder. He continues in an escalation of his mocking style (9), 'It's so UGly'.

Another instance in which Peter uses this mock-serious irony immediately follows the Coliseum discussion that has already been analyzed (p. 72).

(1) Deborah: Did yoù know that where⌉... the statue of Colúmbus
            Steve ╰/?/   ⌋

            is THE center of Manhàttan?

(2) Steve: The gèographical cénter. My bróther told me that

            when I was a lìttle bòy.

(3) Deborah: Your <u>broth</u>er told you? [*laughs*]

               ......

(4) Peter: Ís it reàlly?⌉
(5) David: ⌊God rest his soul. [Deborah *laughs*]

(6) Steve: He also told me about ⌈Fréud.
(7) Deborah: ⌊So I was told.⌉
(8) Peter: ⌊It's the <u>point</u> .... →

(9) Chad: Sex?⌉
(10) Peter: ⌊that .. it's the póint at ⌈which they .... →
(11) Steve: ⌊Freud, Marx <u>and</u> sex.

     Peter: they measure, ... if you say y you're .. thírty-five

            miles from New Yòrk, thàt's where they meán.

(12) Deborah: ⌈It's the center?
(13) Steve: ⌊He didn't tell me about the kind of sex I was

            ínterested in, though.

(14)   Chad: Nnn néver dò.
        [*laughter*]

(15)   Peter: I didn't 'knów.

(16)   Steve: I know. .... Neither did I, actually, to tèll you the trúth.
        [*laughing*]   [Deborah *laughs*]

(17)   Peter: The blìnd leading the blínd.

Steve's statement (2), 'My brother told me that', is ironic because the brother he refers to is sitting next to him, yet he refers to him as if he were not present. David picks up on this when he says (5) 'God rest his soul', as if the brother were not only not present but not alive. Peter then furthers the joke by asking (4) 'Is it really?' as if he did not know what he has just been cited as telling. In keeping with their respective styles, Steve continues the irony in (6), (11), and (13) while Peter continues the geography lesson in (10). When Steve's joke wins out (only I respond to Peter's explanation in [12]), Peter again participates in the irony. However, whereas Steve's utterances (13) and (16) are spoken with laughter, Peter's (15) and (17) are thoroughly deadpan. They are marked for irony in their content and a slight exaggeration in pitch height on their final words.

One final example of Peter's deadpan ironic style will be presented. Peter has made an interpretation of a story told by Steve. I am effusive in my admiration of Peter's interpretation:

(1) Deborah: That's 'grea:t! .... Thát is brilliant.

(2) Steve: ⌐Have yóu ever thought of .... getting a dóctorate in
                        [Deborah & Sally *laugh*- - - - - - - -

           socìology, or psychòlogy?
           - - - - - - - - - - - - - - - -]

           [Deborah *laughs*]

(3) Peter: No.

(4) Steve: Yòu could write a thésis.

(5) Peter: No good jobs.

           [Deborah *chuckles*]

Steve's question (2) is ironic, marked by deliberately emphatic tone, mocking my exaggerated appreciation of Peter's insight. Peter answers in a way that seems deliberately serious: with low voice, relatively low and steady pitch, and reduced syntactic form, in (3) and (5). Only the knowledge that the question was not serious, and the deliberate, clipped quality, make it clear that the answer is not meant seriously either.

Peter does occasionally affect a mocking intonation, but he does so only a few times and always in response to the same usage by others. This was already seen in the sequence in which he picked up Steve's cue to participate in a mock childlike taunting exchange:

> Steve: Do you make things as pretty as I make them?
>
> Peter: Prettier.

To rise to the occasion of Steve's mock challenge, Peter affected a nasal tone and marked downward shift in pitch. But Peter does not initiate such mocking style and does not sustain it for long.

However, Peter is the only person at Thanksgiving who volunteers jokes. One has already been seen (p. 88), the one about the lady who was asked if she smokes after sex. At another point in the conversation, sparked by Chad's reference to a turkey part as 'the pope's nose', Peter asks,

(1) Peter: ⌜Oh, did you héar? The new po- the: new pope, ...

       performed his first míracle?

(2) Chad: What.

(3) David: What. Whatwhatwhat.

(4) Peter: He made a blìnd man láme.

Here too, Peter's humorous style is his serious manner. After he tells this joke, I laugh and David and Chad both comment on the Polish joke. I then say, 'Polish pope, huh,' and Peter repeats, with significantly lowered pitch and no hint of humor, 'A Polish pope. Yeah'. And yet again, after telling this joke, Peter follows up with a genuinely serious explanation: 'That's the <u>neck</u>, by the way. It's not the pope's nose'.

David's humor is similar to Steve's in that he often speaks with an exaggerated form of a speech style. Whereas Steve exaggerates Jewish speech and his own fussiness, David exaggerates stereotypical gay speech patterns; in other words, he camps. At times he speaks with an exaggerated French accent; at other times he overstresses intonational contours. For example, at one point Steve is in the kitchen when the conversation turns to relationships with former spouses and former lovers. When Steve enters the room he asks, with his own mocking style, 'What're we talking about?' Peter answers, 'Relationships'; I say '<u>ex</u>-relationships', and David says, after a slight pause, 'My faw-muh', in response to which everybody laughs. In this rapid succession of comments, each exhibits his or her characteristic style: Steve mocks his own style; Peter answers straight; I slightly alter Peter's comment; and David camps.

Because they share this taste for mocking style, David and Steve sometimes participate in extended 'routines'. For example, at one point reference is made to a dispute that had arisen between Steve and David some time in the past. David begins to explain to the others that they are referring to this past dispute, but before he gets to the end of the sentence, he has taken on an exaggerated intonation pattern and switched the frame of the utterance to 'ironic'. Steve picks up on this, and they have a mock petty argument:

(1) David: We had this big ... we had ... Stéve and I had our
          first fall<u>ing out</u>.⌉
(2) Steve: ⌊First?
(3) David: No. It was .. not our f .. Our thírd. ..... [*laughs*]
          The sécond one was .. [*laughs*] and you remember the
                              [Deborah *laughs*]
(4) Steve: And what about the time be<u>fore</u> the first one.
(5) David: That was ... that was kíndergarten.

As David begins to explain what he and Steve were referring to (1), he sounds serious ('We had this big' ...). However, he hesitates and starts again in a tone that becomes increasingly ironic, until he says 'first falling out' with distinctly emphatic stress. The choice of terms 'falling out' and the exaggerated emphasis mark his tone as ironic. Steve joins the irony by using exaggerated forms of his own style: he latches onto David's statement a clipped, monosyllabic 'First?' Steve's ironic tone in (4) is nasal and rasping, and he maintains it throughout his entire utterance. David, on the other hand, exaggerates emphatic tone but does not use nasalization, and he tends to build up to his full mocking style during his utterance. Furthermore, David laughs in between phrases (3), while Steve maintains the point of view of his mock persona throughout. David's last utterance (5) 'that was ... that was kindergarten.' is spoken in an almost normal tone.

As has already been noted, Chad uses little humor and irony (10 turns in all). Nearly all of his utterances that are ironic are repetitions of or additions to others' irony. These lines are delivered deadpan, that is, in rather standard tones, without exaggerated paralinguistic features. In this, his humorous style resembles Peter's. At another time when David comments ironically on stereotypic gay behavior, Chad says, 'It's genetic.' (This is an extension of the earlier discussion about the gay voice.) In all but one case, Chad's ironic comments are part of a larger ironic interchange such as this.

Sally makes only 7 ironic or humorous statements,[1] but these constitute 4 percent of her utterances as compared to Chad's 2 percent. Sally twice contributes to already established ironic banter, but more often (five times) she offers ironic comments in conversation that is, until that point, serious. For example, there was an extended discussion about theories of learning, in which Steve says that sometimes, when teaching his students, he has to push their fingers to show them what to do; Sally comments, 'And if they still don't respond you take a hammer'. Sally's irony can be very subtle, as when she says, in answer to my question about whether she did the lettering on her flyers, 'I did the lettering and Howard Pyle did the drawing'. Howard Pyle was the cartoonist whose illustrations were borrowed, but he drew his cartoons at the turn of the century; Sally's way of naming him implies that he did the drawings especially for the flyers, with humorous effect. Notice too that while Steve's irony is aimed at mocking his own style, Sally's is content irony; it is aimed outward.[2]

It is important to remember that the forms of humor employed by members of the group on this occasion are not necessarily their only or even standard forms of humor. We can be sure only that this is the way they spoke on this occasion. It is likely, for example, that the fact that he did not know the rest of the participants made Chad more reserved than he might have been with friends. At the same time, someone else might have reacted differently to being the only stranger in the crowd. It is likely too that because Steve was the host, and because his form of humor was paralinguistically gross, that the guests tended to follow his lead in their form of humor. It has been seen that many of the ironic statements were made as part of banter or routines begun by Steve. In fact, in order to make up for this bias, I had Chad and David tape several hours of their private interaction. Although I did not analyze these conversations in detail, in the interest of keeping the data for the present study circumscribed, much of the time during their private interchanges Chad and David engaged in camping and playful routines,

---

[1] It is possible that Sally made statements intended as ironic or humorous which I have not credited her with. For one thing, I may have missed irony where she intended it, and for another, many of her comments are inaudible because she speaks so softly and was seated relatively far from the tape recorder.

[2] Thanks to R. Lakoff for this observation.

in which both participated equally. Their humor there was, however, of a sort somewhat different from what went on at Thanksgiving. It is not appropriate to enter here upon an analysis of their humor on the other occasion. The point to be made is simply that the styles exhibited by participants at Thanksgiving can be understood to represent the behavior they deemed appropriate to the occasion. The use of humor played a significant role in the impact that each had on the group.

CHAPTER 7

Summary of Style Features

The foregoing analysis has attempted to show some of the concrete devices that make up conversational style. The devices that have been illustrated and discussed are, necessarily, only some of the mass of complex devices operating in interaction. As Pittenger et al. (1960:242) note under the function they call *reinforcement*, 'The wise working assumption, then, is always that no matter how many possible contributing factors we have itemized, there may still be others that we have overlooked'. Furthermore, the devices that have been discussed are not discrete phenomena but rather dimensions along which conversational mechanisms operate.

Following is a summary of the dimensions that have been examined.

1. Relative personal focus of topic
2. Paralinguistic features (absolute use and use of marked shifts)
   a. loudness
   b. pitch
   c. pauses
   d. voice quality and tone
3. Expectation that enthusiasm be overtly demonstrated, for example through
   a. quickness of response

    b. paralinguistic features

    c. free offer of related material

    d. use of questions (information, echo, etc.)

4. Use of questions, including

    a. echo questions as back-channel

    b. information questions

5. Pacing

    a. cooperative vs. obstructive overlap

    b. timing of contribution, relative to previous contribution

    c. rate of speech

    d. floor-getting devices (increased amplitude, repetition of words)

6. Use of repetition, for example

    a. to finish other's statement or add to their line of argument

    b. to incorporate other's offer into original statement or argument

7. Topic cohesion (and tolerance for diffuse topics)

8. Tolerance for noise vs. silence

9. Laughter (when, how much)

These and other characteristic ways of saying things are used in the production of specific devices, for example:

1. Machine-gun questions

2. Mutual revelation/personal statements

3. Use of ethnically marked or otherwise ingroup-associated expressions

4. Story rounds

5. Ironic or humorous routines

    The tendency to use such devices based on these dimensions is neither precisely predictable nor random. There are patterns or co-occurrence expectations according to which certain devices tend to cluster, and by which signals in one channel are associated with certain signals in other channels. For example, fast rate of speech; frequent overlap and latching; use of frequent questions; use of high amplitude and high and low pitch, as well as contrasts of these to yield exaggerated contours; tolerance for noise rather than silence—all these were seen to co-occur. (Although this is beyond the scope of the present study, I would hypothesize that these linguistic signals are correlated with such nonverbal factors as use of broad facial expressions and gestures, as well as relatively close kinesic proximity and frequent touching during talk).

Based on their use of these and other devices, the six people gathered for Thanksgiving dinner had styles that were unique in some ways and in others resembled those of other people present to a greater or lesser degree. In some senses, Steve and I shared styles; for example, we tended to talk a lot; we used much overlap, latching, quick expressive responses, and fast, clipped questions. Peter talked less, but he also used overlap, free offer of opinions and thoughts, personal topics, and quick abrupt questions in ways similar to Steve and me. We three told the most stories, and we told nearly all the stories that occurred in rounds. Thus, Peter, Steve, and I seemed to share stylistic strategies, while Chad, David, and Sally differed.

Yet style is not a matter of polar distinctions. Any device can be used to varying degrees, and each person's style is made up of a unique combination of devices. Whereas Steve and I shared pacing strategies, yet his use of humor was more frequent and more extreme than mine. He often initiated comic routines, whereas I often built on others' humor. Steve told more stories, and a greater percentage of his talk was devoted to narrative. He was also more likely to initiate stories unrelated to prior talk. Peter shared many strategies with Steve and me, yet his sense of humor was strikingly different. Peter tended to maintain a serious demeanor and deliver ironic lines in mock sober tones; Steve laughed more and marked ironic statements with exaggerated intonation contours. Peter used expressive paralinguistic features in narratives and plain talk. David, whose pacing devices were very different from those of Steve, Peter and me, exercised a form of humor which resembled Steve's in many ways. Whereas Chad, at first glance, seemed to be using pacing devices similar to David's, it turned out that he did use fast pacing and overlap when the topic was objective rather than personal. He never volunteered personal information, whereas David did; he never contributed stories to rounds, as David did; in fact, he rarely offered stories at all unless he was asked. Chad also used humor much less than David.

Sally, in many ways, was the one whose style was most different. Her voice was the softest; she talked the least. When David and Chad told stories, there was evidence that they did not get to the point in the way that Steve, Peter, and I expected, but when Sally told stories, there was evidence that we could not tell what the point was, nor could David or Chad. Sally's talk showed a relatively high percentage of humor, but the humor was often of a different sort (content rather than style irony).

In other words, each person used a unique mix of conversational devices that constituted individual style. When their devices matched, communication between or among them was smooth. When they differed, communication showed signs of disruption or outright misunderstanding.

Because the present analysis is based on the talk of only six people, it is impossible to draw conclusions about the cultural determination of their styles. Nonetheless it is equally impossible to ignore the fact that those whose styles seemed most similar—especially in the gross outlines, such as turn-taking conventions, use of expressive paralinguistic features, and so on—were of similar ethnic and geographic background. Steve, Peter, and I all grew up in middle class Jewish-identified families and social networks in New York City. (The fact that Steve and I met in summer camp when we were teenagers is evidence that our families had similar orientations.) Chad and David, on the other hand, grew up in sections of Southern California which were not ethnic identified. Chad, however, was less disconcerted by the fast pace of the evening's talk, and he was better able to participate. One cannot help but wonder whether the fact that his mother is an Italian from New York City plays a part in this difference.

The one who was least able to participate in terms of rhythm and the establishment of thematic cohesion was Sally, who was born and raised in England. Moreover, anyone who has experience with people from the backgrounds represented in this group immediately identifies the devices used by the New Yorkers in this group as somehow reminiscent of the styles they have observed in people from that background, and of Sally's style as somehow typical of upper-class British speech.

It is certainly not the case that anyone from these backgrounds talks just like this. People differ in individual ways. Nonetheless, use of such conversational devices and the expectation that others will use them is certainly learned the way language is learned, i.e. in interaction with family and friends. Although there is no inherent disposition toward particular stylistic devices associated with ethnicity or class, ethnic and other subcultural identification often involves one in social networks in which particular linguistic strategies are exercised and thereby learned

(Gumperz 1982b). It would be surprising indeed if people who habitually interacted with each other did not develop ways of talking that became generalized among them.

Conversational style, then, may be seen as a mix of devices made up of features and used according to strategies for serving the human needs for interpersonal involvement and independence. In one sense, each device is represented by a kind of continuum. Speakers may be distributed on one continuum with respect to how fast they pace their comments relative to previous comments; another for how gross their paralinguistic features are; another for how many stories they tell, and so on. In this sense, speakers in the Thanksgiving group occupy different places on different continua. A continuum representing grossness of styles of humor might look like this:

A continuum representing pacing practices might look something like this:

Percentage of talk devoted to stories yields this:

But numbers of narratives told yields yet another:

If these continua are superimposed one upon the other, perhaps some overall continuum representing relative signaling of involvement and considerateness would yield something like this:[1]

Considerateness ———————————————————————— Involvement

An interesting insight is suggested by the different ways in which the people in this group of speakers perceived each other. In recalling the occasion several months after it had occurred, Sally had referred to the group as a 'rambunctious crowd', and she identified the participants of that crowd as Steve, Peter, David, and me. David, in contrast, thought the evening was dominated by Steve, Peter, and me. Peter thought the evening was dominated by Steve, and Steve thought it was dominated by me. I had the impression that Steve, Peter, and I had participated equally, to the exclusion of the other three.

Reference to the considerateness/involvement continuum may account for this discrepancy.[2] Discriminations among speakers become more refined, the closer one is to those speakers in style. Thus, to Sally, David's style was more like the styles of the rest of us than like her own, so she perceived him in association with us. To David, it was clear that Peter, Steve, and I differed from himself, so he did not make distinctions among our styles. Peter, however, is very familiar with fast-talking style, and he thus perceived differences between Steve and me. Steve, on the other hand, might be disinclined to see himself as dominating, so he naturally perceived the one with the next grossest style in that role.

It seems likely, considering my findings, that some aspects of style are particularly salient: pacing, grossness of humor, story-telling. It seems likely that Steve and I perceived David as more active a participant than he was because he told a number of long stories and because he joked a lot, with a paralinguistically gross style. Similarly, we per-

---

[1]Kochman (1981) identifies similar opposing values as the rights of feelings vs. the rights of sensibilities, corresponding to my involvement/considerateness (or independence) principles. He finds that differing values placed on these rights account for Black/White style differences. The present study suggests that White style is not monolithic.

[2]Robin Lakoff alerted me to this perspective, by suggesting the continuum and observing the operating principle, "anyone to the right of me is rambunctious."

ceived Peter as more active a participant than he was because he kept up with the fast pace and told many stories.

Conversational style, then, is made up of use of specific devices, chosen by reference to broad operating principles or conversational strategies. The use of these devices is habitual and may be more or less automatic. The goal of all conversation is to make clear to others the intentions of the speaker; the degree to which one's meaning is understood as intended depends upon the degree to which conversational strategies, and hence use of devices, are similar. Furthermore, the similarity of such devices makes for rhythmically smooth interaction. Both the rhythmic synchrony and the construction of shared meaning create the satisfying sense of harmony that often accompanies conversation among people who share social, ethnic, geographic, or class background. By the same token, the use of strategies and consequent devices that are not understood or expected creates a sense of dissonance, which often leads to negative or mistaken judgments of intent. This, in turn, often leads one to walk away from an encounter feeling dissatisfied or disgruntled. Thus an understanding of conversational style explains in part what often appears as clannishness among members of certain groups, or discrimination or prejudice on the part of others.

The present study has focused on a single extended interaction, during which a particular style in some way 'dominated'. Although all conversational devices can be successful when used by speakers who share expectations of signaling systems, it is in the nature of interaction that when devices are not the same, one style takes over. For example, those who expect shorter pauses between utterances will necessarily speak first; having spoken, they effectively block the contributions of others, but just those others who cannot tolerate much overlap. The voices of those who talk more loudly than their interlocutors in a given interaction will necessarily ring out, and the voices of those who talk more softly will, thereby, be drowned out or overshadowed. These effects are independent of the intentions of the speakers involved. Thus, the fastest-paced speakers in any group are the ones that will be observed to talk the most.

This has been a first attempt to describe the features and devices that constitute conversational style. Much work remains to be done to continue such description, to understand better the strategies and universal principles underlying them, to document the devices that make up different styles, to investigate styles in different contexts and in interaction with each other, to correlate linguistic with nonverbal channels of communication and nonlinguistic aspects of behavior.

The study of conversational style, moreover, is no more nor less than the study of communication. The features that make up conversational style are the conventions by which meaning is communicated in social interaction. Differences in conversational style contribute to the phenomenon that Becker (1982:3) discusses, paraphrasing Ortega y Gasset to the effect that all utterances are both 'deficient' and 'exuberant'. They fail to communicate precisely and entirely what one intends, and they communicate more than one intends, including, as has been demonstrated in the Thanksgiving interaction, images of oneself.

Understanding conversational style, then, is a matter of identifying the system linking aspects of discourse realization and organization, as well as linking this linguistic system to other aspects of human behavior and consciousness. In this sense, the study of style is the study of coherence. The following and final chapter suggests some of the processes that create coherence in conversation, further investigation of which may give direction to future research.

CHAPTER 8

The Study of Coherence in Discourse

The experience of a perfectly tuned conversation is like an artistic experience. The satisfaction of shared rhythm, shared appreciation of nuance, mutual understanding that surpasses the meaning of words exchanged (such as has been illustrated in the interchanges between the Thanksgiving participants who shared stylistic strategies), goes beyond the pleasure of having one's message understood. It is a ratification of one's way of being human and proof of connection to other people. It gives a sense of coherence in the world. Becker (1979) defines an aesthetic response as one in which discourse constraints are perceived as coherent. In this sense, successful conversation is an aesthetic experience.

In contrast, unsuccessful conversation is maddening. As has been seen in the effects on the Thanksgiving conversation of participants' differing stylistic strategies, the inability to establish shared rhythm makes it impossible to exchange speaking turns smoothly. When one's intentions are repeatedly misinterpreted, and when one cannot see the coherence in others' behavior, one begins to lose a sense of coherence in the world. This is the trauma of cross-cultural communication, and the appellation *cross-cultural* may apply in far more situations than one would initially assume or wish.

An understanding of the basis of coherence in conversation is needed for an understanding of human interaction. I like to think of the study of coherence as an aesthetics of conversation, in Becker's sense of coherence and aesthetics. I believe that such understanding may grow out of an analysis of conversation in the spirit and tradition that has hitherto been applied to literary language.

I would like to suggest that literary language, rather than being maximally different from ordinary conversation, builds on and intensifies features that are spontaneous and commonplace in ordinary conversation because both depend for their effect on what Havelock (1963) and Ong (1967) call subjective knowing.

Bearing in mind that the distinction between objective and subjective knowing is an idealization for heuristic purposes—no form of discourse is devoid of logic or of emotion—it is instructive to consider Havelock's (1963) suggestion that Plato sought to ban poets from educational processes in *The Republic* because they dangerously inspired people to subjective knowing by establishing in the audience a sense of identification with the poet or the characters in the epic. In contrast, objective knowing is the result of logical processes that Havelock associates with literacy, but I believe are better understood as growing out of relatively less focus on interpersonal involvement and more on message content (Tannen in press-a).

Conversation, like epic poetic performance, derives its impact from processes of identification between audience and speaker, to similar ends. In other words, face to face conversation, like literature, seeks primarily to MOVE an audience by means of involvement, as opposed to (typically) expository prose (in Havelock's terms, literacy), which seeks to CONVINCE an audience while maintaining distance between speaker/writer and audience. Of course, different types of face-to-face conversation differ with respect to relative focus on interpersonal involvement. For example, casual conversation at a social gathering would typically entail more interpersonal involvement than directions given in answer to a request by a stranger.

In light of this hypothesis, I will conclude this book on conversational style with the suggestion that future research (my own and that of interested others) focus on elucidating the relationship between various discourse genres, and that a good starting place is an understanding of the relationship between ordinary conversation and literary discourse. Toward that beginning, I will outline some of the features that have been identified in literary language, which I suggest are basic to conversation. Evidence for this suggestion can be gathered from scattered research findings in a number of fields, including anthropology, sociology, rhetoric, linguistics, psychology, and artificial intelligence. I will present these features grouped in the following categories:

1. rhythm
2. surface linguistic features
3. contextualization including
   a. ellipsis (called implicature or indirectness in conversation)
   b. figures of speech
   c. imagery and detail

In each of these categories, I will indicate briefly how conversation can be seen to exhibit features that have been identified as quintessentially literary. Because this concluding section is presented in the spirit of directions for future research rather than research already undertaken, the illustrations will necessarily be decidedly brief, and more often than not, taken from others' research rather than my own. I will suggest, finally, that the reason for this similarity lies in the fact that the features contribute to processes of subjective knowing, or speaker/writer-audience involvement.

Rhythm

Rhythm has long been seen as basic to poetry and literary prose. The cadence of the language sweeps the audience along, literally moving them to share the author's point of view. Recent research establishes that rhythm is as basic to conversation as it is to music and poetry. Erickson and Shultz (1982) demonstrate that successful conversation can be set to a metronome; movements and utterances are synchronized and carried out on the beat. This phenomenon is informally observed when, following a pause, two speakers begin speaking at precisely the same moment, or when two people suddenly move—for example, crossing their legs or shifting their weight—at the same moment and often in the same direction. Even more remarkable is the work of Condon (for example, Condon 1963) on rhythmic microsynchrony, demonstrating that, when cultural background is shared, speakers' and hearers' utterances and movements begin within the same frame of a movie film.

Scollon (1982) corroborates the finding that conversation is carried out in rhythm and suggests that the dominant duple rhythm may result from the human heartbeat. This may underlie a metaphoric and also real association between the rhythmic basis of interaction and the feeling of being moved to subjective knowing. That is, the rhythmic synchrony basic to conversational interaction contributes to participant involvement much as singing along or tapping one's foot in rhythm with music. The opposite experience—lack of involvement resulting from inability to share rhythm—can be envisioned in the experience of trying to clap along but continually missing the beat.

Surface Linguistic Features

Many literary scholars have recognized as basic to literature recurrent patterns of sound (for example, alliteration, assonance, rhyme), words, syntactic constructions, and discourse structures. I suggest that sound and structural patterns, like rhythm, serve to sweep the audience along toward subjective knowing. Once again, scattered findings by researchers in linguistics, sociology, artificial intelligence, and anthropology indicate that these features are spontaneous in ordinary conversation. The work of Harvey Sacks (for example, Sacks 1971) demonstrates that spontaneous conversation uses repetition of sounds and words (what he called sound and lexical touchoffs, or sound selection). He suggests, for example, that a conversational analyst, in determining why a speaker chooses one or another phonological variant of a lexical item (in a case he discusses, 'because', 'cause', or 'cuz'), should look to see if the variant chosen is 'sound coordinated with things in its environment'. In his example, a speaker says, referring to fish, 'cause it comes from cold water', and a few lines later says, 'You better eat something because you're gonna be hungry before we get there'. In suggesting why 'cause' occurs in the first instance and 'because' in the second, Sacks notes that 'cause' appears in the environment of repeated /k/ sounds, whereas 'because' is coordinated with *be* in 'be hungry' and 'before'.

Ochs (1979), Winograd (1976), and Tannen (1982) observe repetition of syntactic constructions in spoken narratives. For example, in my own study, I found a speaker spontaneously saying, about a fellow worker, 'And he knows Spanish, and he knows French, and he knows English, and he knows German . . .' Her story depends for its impact on the recurrent syntactic pattern 'and he knows . . .', both in its establishment and in its final violation.

Bright (1982), following Tedlock and Hymes, shows that American Indian spoken discourse contains verbal particles that mark verse structure in what was not previously thought to be poetry. In English, Chafe (1980) finds verbal markers of sentence and episode boundaries in oral narrative: 'and', 'and uh', 'and then', 'anyway', and measurable pauses are all systematic and mark discourse structures similar to verse structure in poetry. I suggest that this conforming to familiar structural patterns makes the discourse sound or feel 'right', and this sense of rightness is then transferred from the structure to the content. Hence, Havelock's assumption that poets held an undeserved power to influence their audiences.

Contextualization

Rader (1982) demonstrates that in written literature crucial information is omitted that must be supplied by the reader to make sense of a text. As she puts it, the reader creates a world according to the writer's instructions, and this filling in by the reader of necessary context (hence the term 'contextualization') is basic to the literary process. This process is present, to some extent, in all discourse. No text would be comprehensible without considerable shared context and background knowledge, as a number of scholars have observed (for example, Fillmore 1976, Prince 1981). However, the filling in of background information is maximal in literary language, the most dramatic example being poetry, in which the goal is to evoke the most elaborate sets of associations in the reader by use of the sparest verbal representation. In short stories, novels, and plays, as well, the writers' skills are often judged by their ability to communicate much information about their characters and their worlds in just a few words or lines.

This process of contextualization is basic as well to conversation. Nearly all conversational analysts have observed that most casual conversation, if transcribed and considered by itself, appears incoherent (for example, Labov and Fanshel 1977). In effect, in casual talk, everyone speaks what Bernstein (1964) calls 'restricted code', using references not fully explained or elaborated in the discourse but recoverable from the immediate context or prior knowledge.

As I have discussed and demonstrated in the analysis of the conversational strategies of the Thanksgiving celebrants, and as R. Lakoff has repeatedly argued (for example, Lakoff 1976), speakers do not ordinarily say what they mean. They prefer indirectness, for two reasons: to save face if their opinions or wants are not favorably received, and to achieve the sense of rapport that comes from being understood without saying what one means. In addition, I suggest, indirectness in conversation, by requiring the listener to fill in unstated information, simultaneously contributes to the process of subjective knowing by engendering audience participation in sense making. Indirectness in conversation is a way of saying one thing and meaning another. This entails that some of the work of supplying meaning is done by the hearer. People value more highly achievements they have worked to accomplish. Just so, this hearer filling-in contributes to subjective knowing, or understanding through involvement, much like contextualization in literature.

Literary critics have identified the use in literature of numerous linguistic devices that I would like to suggest have the effect of requiring audience participation in sense making, or contextualization. These devices include (1) ellipsis (2) figures of speech and (3) imagery and detail.

Ellipsis

If indirectness is a way of saying one thing and meaning another, ellipsis is a way of saying nothing and meaning something. This device, which has been studied extensively in literary texts, is the same phenomenon that has been studied in linguistics as implicature, or indirectness. What meaning is derived that is not explicitly stated in the text? In the classic linguistic example of an indirect speech act, the statement 'It's cold in here' may communicate a message about a window without ever mentioning a window.

Figures of Speech

Much literary criticism has investigated the use of various tropes, or figures of speech, such as the following (most of these are mentioned in Friedrich 1979):

irony (see also Roy 1978)
enigma (riddles)
parimia (speaking in proverbs)
allegory
parable
metaphor (meaning transferred by analogy)
metonym (meaning transferred to an associated notion; e.g. 'sword' for 'war')
synecdoche (the part for the whole or vice versa; e.g. 'greybeard' for old man, or 'the law' for 'policeman'.

All of these figures of speech are ways of saying one thing and meaning another. Most of them are what Friedrich (1979) calls 'analogically based'. That is, they derive meaning not from the logical processes of induction and deduction but from what Bateson (1979) calls 'abduction': the 'lateral extension of abstract components of description'. Abduction is a cognitive leap from one descriptive system to another by way of abstract, not linear links.

These figures of speech, which have long been recognized as the stuff of which literature is made, are also commonplace, though sometimes less artfully developed, in ordinary conversation.

For example, Sacks (1971) demonstrates that choice of words in ordinary conversation is often the result of metaphoric associations. Posing the question why a woman says to her husband the oddly formal, 'Will you be good enough to empty this in there,' Sacks suggests that her choice of the expression 'be good enough' is metaphorically conditioned by the environment of several other measure terms: 'empty' in the cited expression, and 'more' and 'missing' in nearby sentences. Others have observed as well that metaphor is basic to everyday talk (Friedrich 1979, Lakoff and Johnson 1980).

Imagery and Detail

Concrete images and specific details are widely assumed to be basic to imaginative literature. These too, I suggest, contribute to subjective knowing; in response to their immediacy and vividness, readers conjure up associations based on their own prior experience. Chafe (1982), in comparing spoken and written narratives, finds that stories told spontaneously in ordinary conversation are characterized by use of specific details and 'imageability'.

All of these findings indicate that ordinary conversation operates on principles and processes that have been studied in literary language. My hypothesis is that literary language makes increased and artful use of features that are spontaneous in face-to-face conversation because both rely for their effect on processes of subjective knowing, that is, speaker/writer-audience involvement.

Conclusion

The investigation of coherence in discourse is an inquiry into the nature of human cognition and communication. Friedrich (1979) considers the relationship between poetry and conversation as part of an analysis aimed at redefining the Whorf Hypothesis. He concludes, 'It is the more poetic levels and processes of language, however defined, that massively model, constrain, trigger, and otherwise affect the individual imagination' (p. 473).

Poetic processes include many features that have been demonstrated in the conversational strategies of the Thanksgiving participants, as well as those outlined in the present chapter. It shall remain for future research to discover more precisely what these poetic processes are, and how they work toward coherence in conversation. It will be useful to ask, for example, with regard to sample texts in disparate genres,

1. Which of the identified features are used?
2. With what frequency are they used?
3. How are they introduced?
4. How are they developed?
5. For what purpose in the discourse or the context are they used?
6. Are there comparable patterns and uses of features in discourse of various genres (for example, narrative, joking, description, directions)?

Tyler (1978:167) argues that the 'separation of reason and passion has destroyed the ethical basis of discourse'. In a similar vein, Powers (1981) recommends that linguists consider Susanne Langer's observations that modern scientific investigations have failed to take into account the basic matter of human feeling. The study of discourse can be looked to to bridge this gap. We can undertake rigorous analysis of linguistic form, and we must keep always in sight the goal of understanding the effects of such form on the people who use discourse in their daily lives. Processes of producing and understanding discourse are matters of human feeling and human interaction. An understanding of these processes in language will contribute to a rational as well as ethical and humane basis for understanding what it means to be human.

APPENDIX I

Steps in Analyzing Conversation

1. Tape record (with consent) interactions whenever possible. Choose one to study—one that is very familiar or very intriguing, but one preferably with identifiable boundaries and including participants you can later interview. (Avoid overly personal or emotional interactions, unless you have a special reason for choosing such and feel qualified to deal with the repercussions.)
2. What speech event is taking place? What is the tone (what Hymes calls the 'key') of the interaction?
3. Identify rough spots or otherwise marked segments such as (a) miscommunication, or what Erickson calls 'uncomfortable moments' (perhaps where a participant has later commented, 'something was funny there'), or (b) a segment that seems particularly pleasing ('there we were really clicking—that was a perfect conversation'), or (c) a segment representative of some characteristic that has been noticed ('That's what always happens').
4. Closely study that segment. Listen to it again and again. Transcribe it. What is going on there? Look for such linguistic phenomena as words spoken, propositions, topics: which ones, how are they introduced, how are they maintained; paralinguistic and prosodic features: pauses, pitch, loudness; turntaking, overlap, interruption.
5. Compare the features found in the identified segment with those found in other segments of the interaction.
6. Count: words, pauses, topics, overlaps, etc.

7. Diagram: outline topics, propositions, patterns of agreement and disagreement, etc.
8. Get the reactions and interpretations of participants after the fact.
9. Get the reactions and interpretations of nonparticipants.
10. Try your own interpretations and those gleaned from (7) and (8) on colleagues and nonlinguist friends.
11. Try your interpretations out in the academic or the real world.
12. See if the hypotheses generated shed light on other data (or on life).

APPENDIX II

Participants in Thanksgiving Dinner

SETTING: the dining room of Steve's home in Berkeley, California.

TIME: Thanksgiving, 1978.

PARTICIPANTS:

Steve, 33, the host at his home in Berkeley, California; musician and music teacher; born and raised in the Bronx, New York.

Peter, 35, Steve's brother, a management analyst at a university; born and raised in the Bronx; lives in the East Bay, California.

Sally, 29, lived with Steve from 1970 until 1976; musician; lives in Canada; born and raised in London, England.

David, 29, Steve's friend since 1974; artist and sign language interpreter; lives in Berkeley, California; born and raised in Riverside, California.

Chad, 30, David's friend since they met as university students in 1972; writer for a major film production studio; born and raised in Los Angeles, California.

Deborah, 33, Steve's friend since they met at summer camp in 1959; graduate student in linguistics at University of California, Berkeley; lives in Berkeley; born and raised in Brooklyn, New York. Also the author.

Seating Arrangement

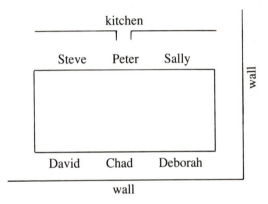

APPENDIX III

Flow of Topics in Thanksgiving Conversation[1]

Tape 1 Side A   (First Hour)

Digital Counter	Topic	Participants	How it came up
1 20 40 60	men/women	all	Steve: She's such a little girl already. (about photo of niece)
80 100	adoption	all	Peter mentions article read in journal
120	Loud family	all (Chad, Steve)	David: Speaking of which . . .
140 160 180	Goffman	Deborah Chad Peter Steve (Sally)	Chad: That's like Erving Goffman kind of stuff.

[1]When necessary, names are abbreviated: De = Deborah, St = Steve, Da = David, Ch = Chad, Sa = Sally, P = Peter. If there is a main speaker, his/her name is in caps. If there are speakers who participated but little, their names are in parentheses. See also Table 2, Chapter Three for number of words spoken by each participant per episode. Digital counter refers to timing as reflected in digital counter on tape recorder.

Digital Counter	Topic	Participants	How it came up
200 220	lifestyle	Deborah Peter	Deborah: Do you read?
240			
260 280 300 320 340 360 380 400 420	The Whorf Hypothesis	Chad Deborah (Peter) David	Chad: We were talking about this last night too, that . . . somebody had a theory that um language the syntax of the language you're in and and its grammar and laws and all those kinds of things and the words prescribe the way that you think.
440 460 480 500 520 540	Los Angeles	Chad Deborah	Deborah: You live in LA?
560 580 600 620 640 660	sitting down to dinner	Peter Chad Deborah (Sally) (David) (Steve serving)	(all talk) Peter: Should I carve the turkey at the table or here?

Tape 1 Side A   (First Hour) *Continued*

Digital Counter	Topic	Participants	How it came up
680 — 700 —	holidays	Sally, Deborah, Peter (Steve, David)	Deborah (to Sally): Have you internalized Thanksgiving?
720 —	tape recorder	St, De, Da, Ch	St: Do we have to have this here?
	wine	Ch, Da, P (St)	(Steve serving)
740 —	organizations	P, De, (Ch, Sa, Da)	P: I got in the mail the other day
760 780 800 820 840 860 880 900 920 940	food	all	David: Sally, you know what? The Joy of Cooking says about uh ratatouille?

Tape 1 Side B (Second Hour)

Digital Counter	Topic	Participants	How it came up
1	bagels	St, Sa, De, Da	Sally: the meal on the airplane
20	Ch's NY trip	Da, De, St, P (Ch)	Chad: That's what I expected
40	NY geography	St, De, P	Steve: Dju go to the west side
60 80 100 120	Chad's job	Peter Steve Chad David Deborah	Peter: You never met [name]?
140	(hands)	(Deborah, Sally)	
160 180 200	cartoons	all	Peter: Somebody was saying they thought he was a real sadist. Towards kids. Deborah: /That's right./ The cartoons are pretty sadistic.
220	Quonset huts	St, P, De	St: We got a tv in the quonset hut
240 260 280 300 320 340	camp	STEVE Deborah (Peter) (Chad) (David)	Steve: And HIS son went to my camp
360 380	school	PETER, De (Ch, St)	Peter: Yknow like we're sending Jonny to private school now
400	social class	DEBORAH P, St, (Sa)	Peter: tracking in school and social class
420	coffee	P, St, Da, De	Peter: Maybe I'll have coffee.

167

Tape 1 Side B (Second Hour) *Continued*

Digital Counter	Topic	Participants	How it came up
440			
460			
480			
500		DAVID	Steve: [to David]
520	sign language	Deborah (Steve) (Peter)	How do you say "discrete"? [in sign]
540		(Chad) (Sally)	
560			
580			
600			
620			
640			
660	freak accidents	DEBORAH Peter Sally	Deborah: I read something . . .
680		Steve Chad	
700			
720	finishing dinner	all	Peter: We don't have anything for dessert.
740			
760			
780		PETER	Peter: It's so interesting. Like uh leaving a relationship and
800	relationships	Deborah (David)	being with people who respond differently. Yknow
820		(Sally) (Steve)	
840		(Chad)	
860			

Tape 1 Side B   (Second Hour) *Continued*

Digital Counter	Topic	Participants	How it came up
880		PETER	
900	kids & sex	Deborah (Steve)	Peter: What I think about is my children
920		(David)	
940			

Tape 2 Side A   (Last 40 minutes)

Digital Counter	Topic	Participants	How it came up
1 20	(Continuation of discussion of book Chad and Peter have read)		
40			(Change of tape -- ??)
60	learning	all but David	
80			
100			
120	piano hands	Steve, Deborah Sally, David (Ch)	Steve (to Chad): You have a better hand for the piano than I
140	scolding	STEVE, De	Steve: I tell my students . . .
160	tickets	STEVE, all	Steve: How many ya want, Peter?
180	postdinner talk	CHAD, St, Da, De, Sa	Steve: Would you like a cushion?
200	smoking	Peter, Deborah Chad	Peter: I wouldn't mind tobacco
220 240	pig story	SALLY, Da, De	Sally: It's a wonderful poem . . .

Tape 2   Side A   (Last 40 Minutes) *Continued*

Digital Counter	Topic	Participants	How it came up
260			Steve offers drinks
280	after-dinner drinks	all (Chad) (in various combinations)	
300			
320	(mixed talk)		
340			
360			
380			Steve: bilingual pun on some- one's name
400			
420			
440	words	Steve Deborah David (Peter) (Chad)	
460			
480			
500			

Tape 2   Side B

Digital Counter	Topic	Participants	How it came up
1 / 20	words (continued)	Steve, Deborah David (Peter)	(?—continued from off tape)
40 / 60	homosexuality (2 parallel conversations)	DAVID Deborah/Sally	Da: Oh I have to tell you about

APPENDIX IV

Further Readings in Sociolinguistics

Books:

Bolinger, Dwight. 1981. Language: The loaded weapon. London: Longman.

Fasold, Ralph. In press. The sociolinguistics of society. London: Blackwell.

Fasold, Ralph. In preparation. The sociolinguistics of language. London: Blackwell.

Giglioli, Pier Paolo. 1972. Language and social context. Baltimore, MD: Penguin.

Green, Judith, and Cynthia Wallat (eds.). 1981. Ethnography and language in educational settings. Norwood, NJ: Ablex.

Gumperz, John J. 1982. Discourse strategies. London: Cambridge U. Press.

Gumperz, John J. (ed.). 1982. Language and social identity. Cambridge: Cambridge U. Press.

Gumperz, John J., and Dell Hymes (eds.). 1972. Directions in sociolinguistics. New York: Holt Rinehart Winston.

Hymes, Dell. 1974. Foundations in sociolinguistics. Philadelphia: University of Pennsylvania.

Saville-Troike, Muriel. 1982. The ethnography of communication. London: Blackwell.

Shuy, Roger (ed.). 1973. Sociolinguistics: Current trends and prospects. 23rd Annual Round Table. Washington, DC: Georgetown U. Press.

Trudgill, Peter. 1972. Sociolinguistics. Baltimore, MD: Penguin.

APPENDIX V

Further Readings in Discourse Analysis

Part I: Conversation

Books:

Coulthard, Malcolm. 1977. An introduction to discourse analysis. London: Longmans.
Gumperz, John J. 1982. Discourse strategies. London: Cambridge U. Press.
Labov, William, & David Fanshel. 1977. Therapeutic discourse. New York: Academic Press.
Lakoff, Robin. 1975. Language and woman's place. New York: Harper & Row.
Tannen, Deborah (ed.). 1982. Analyzing discourse: Text and talk, Georgetown University Round Table on Languages and Linguistics 1981. Washington DC: Georgetown U. Press.

Articles:

Brown, Penelope, and Stephen Levinson. 1978. Universals in language usage: Politeness phenomena. Questions and politeness, ed. by Esther Goody, 56–289. Cambridge: Cambridge U. Press.
Ekman, Paul. 1979. About brows: Emotional and conversational signals. Human ethology, ed. by M. von Cranach, K. Foppa, W. Lepenies, & D. Ploog, 169–249. Cambridge: Cambridge U. Press.
Fillmore, Charles J. 1979. On fluency. Individual differences in language ability and language behavior, ed. by Charles J. Fillmore, Daniel Kempler, & William S.-Y. Wang, 85–101. New York: Academic Press.
Goffman, Erving. 1967. The nature of deference and demeanor. Interaction Ritual, 47–95. Garden City, New York: Doubleday.
Goffman, Erving. 1981. Footing. Forms of talk, 124–159. Philadelphia: U. of Pennsylvania Press.
Lakoff, Robin. 1973. The logic of politeness, or minding your p's and q's. Papers from the Ninth Regional Meeting of the Chicago Linguistics Society, 292–305.

Lakoff, Robin. 1979. Stylistic strategies within a grammar of style. Language, sex, and gender, ed. by Judith Orasanu, Mariam Slater, & Leonore Loeb Adler. Annals of the New York Academy of Science 327.53–78.

Sacks, Harvey. 1971. Unpublished lecture notes, March 11, 1971.

Sacks, Harvey, and Emanuel Schegloff. 1974. Opening up closings. Ethnomethodology, ed. by Roy Turner. Baltimore, MD: Penguin.

Shultz, Jeffrey, Susan Florio, and Frederick Erickson. 1982. Where's the floor? Aspects of the cultural organization of social relationships in communication at home and at school. Ethnography and education: Children in and out of school, ed. by Perry Gilmore & Alan Glatthorn, 88–123. Washington, DC: Center for Applied Linguistics.

Soskin, William F., and Vera P. John. 1963. The study of spontaneous talk. The stream of behavior, ed. by Roger Barker, 228–281. New York: Appleton-Century-Crofts.

Part II: Narrative and Spoken/Written Language

Books:

Bartlett, Frederick C. 1932. Remembering. Cambridge: Cambridge U. Press.

Propp, Vladimir. 1958. Morphology of the folktale. Austin, TX: U. of Texas Press.

Tannen, Deborah (ed.). 1982. Spoken and written language: Exploring orality and literacy. Norwood, NJ: Ablex.

Articles:

Bloodgood, Fred 'Doc'. 1982. The medicine and sideshow pitches. Analyzing discourse: Text and talk, Georgetown University Round Table on Languages and Linguistics 1981, ed. by Deborah Tannen, 371–382. Washington DC: Georgetown U. Press.

Bolinger, Dwight. 1976. Meaning and memory. Forum Linguisticum 1:1. 1–14.

Chafe, Wallace. 1980. The deployment of consciousness in the production of a narrative. The pear stories: Cognitive, cultural, and linguistic aspects of narrative production, ed. by Wallace Chafe, 9–50. Norwood, NJ: Ablex.

Fillmore, Charles J. 1976. The need for a frame semantics within linguistics. Statistical methods in linguistics, 5–29. Stockholm: Skriptor.

Goody, Jack, and Ian Watt. 1963. The consequences of literacy. Comparative studies in society and history 5.304–345. (Reprinted in Giglioli, Language and social context.)

Kay, Paul. 1977. Language evolution and speech style. Sociocultural dimensions of language change, ed. by Ben Blount & Mary Sanches, 21–33. New York: Academic Press.

Labov, William. 1972. The transformation of experience in narrative syntax. Language in the inner city, 354–396. Philadelphia: U. of Pennsylvania Press.

Nystrand, Martin. 1982. Rhetoric's "audience" and linguistics' "speech community": Implications for understanding writing and text. What writers know: The language, process, and structure of written discourse, 1–28. New York: Academic Press.

Ochs, Elinor. 1979. Planned and unplanned discourse. Discourse and syntax, ed. by Talmy Givon, 51–80. New York: Academic.

Olson, David. 1977. From utterance to text: The bias of language in speech and writing. Harvard Educational Review 47:3. 257–281.

Ong, Walter J. 1979. Literacy and orality in our times. Profession 79. 1–7.

Polanyi, Livia. 1978. False starts can be true. Proceedings of the Fourth Annual Meeting of the Berkeley Linguistics Society, 628–639.

Polanyi, Livia. 1979. So what's the point? Semiotica 25:3/4. 207–241.

Tannen, Deborah. 1979. What's in a frame? Surface evidence for underlying expectations. New directions in discourse processing, ed. by Roy Freedle, 137–181. Norwood, NJ: Ablex.

Tannen, Deborah. 1980. A comparative analysis of oral narrative strategies. The pear stories: Cognitive, cultural, and linguistic aspects of narrative production, ed. by Wallace Chafe, 51–87. Norwood, NJ: Ablex.

Further Readings in Cross-cultural Communication

Videotapes

Gumperz, John J., and the National Industrial Language Training Centre, Middlesex, England. Crosstalk.

Scollon, Ron, and Eliza Jones. Talking Alaska. Alaska Native Language Center, U. of Alaska, Fairbanks.

Books:

Erickson, Frederick, and Jeffrey Shultz. 1982. Gatekeeping in counseling interviews. New York: Academic.

Forster, E. M. 1924. A passage to India. New York: Harcourt, Brace.

Gumperz, John J. (ed.). 1982. Language and social identity. Cambridge: Cambridge U. Press.

Kochman, Thomas. 1981. Black and white styles in conflict. Chicago: U. of Chicago Press.

Lakoff, Robin. 1975. Language and woman's place. New York: Harper & Row.

Tannen, Deborah (ed.). 1984. Coherence in spoken and written discourse. Norwood, NJ: Ablex.

Articles:

Becker, A. L. 1979. Text-building, epistemology, and aesthetics in Javanese Shadow Theatre. The imagination of reality, ed. by A. L. Becker & Aram Yengoyan, 211–243. Norwood, NJ: Ablex.

Erickson, Frederick. 1979. Talking down: Some cultural sources of miscommunication in interracial interviews. Nonverbal behavior, ed. by Aaron Wolfgang, 99–126. New York: Academic Press.

Freedman, Daniel. 1979. Ethnic differences in babies. Human Nature, January 1979. 37–43.

Guilmet, George M. 1979. Maternal perceptions of urban Navajo and Caucasian children's classroom behavior. Human Organization 38:1. 87–91.

Gumperz, John J. 1978. The conversational analysis of interethnic communication. Interethnic communication, ed. by E. Lamar Ross, 13–31. Southern Anthropological Society Proceedings, No. 12. Athens, GA: U. of Georgia Press.

Kempton, Willet. 1980. The rhythmic basis of interactional microsynchrony. Verbal and nonverbal communication, ed. by Mary Ritchie Key. The Hague: Mouton.

Michaels, Sarah, and Jenny Cook-Gumperz. 1979. A study of sharing time with first grade children. Proceedings of Fifth Annual Meeting of the Berkeley Linguistics Society. Berkeley, California: Department of Linguistics, Berkeley, California, 647–659.

Philips, Susan U. 1972. Participant structures and communicative competence: Warm Springs children in community and classroom. Functions of Language in the Classroom, ed. by Courtney Cazden, Vera John, and Dell Hymes, 370–394. New York: Teachers College Press.

Saville-Troike, Muriel. 1980. Cross-cultural communication in the classroom. Current issues in bilingual education, Georgetown University Round Table on Languages and Linguistics 1980, ed. by James E. Alatis, 348–355. Washington, DC: Georgetown U. Press.

Scollon, Ron, and Suzanne B. K. Scollon. 1981. Athabaskan English interethnic communication. Narrative, literacy, and face in interethnic communication, 11–37. Norwood, NJ: Ablex.

Tannen, Deborah. 1980. Implications of the oral/literate continuum for cross-cultural communication. Current issues in bilingual education, Georgetown University Round Table on Languages and Linguistics 1980, ed. by James E. Alatis, 326–347. Georgetown U. Press.

References

Agar, Michael. 1975. Cognition and events. Sociocultural dimensions of language use, ed. by Mary Sanches & Ben Blount, 41–56. New York: Academic Press.

Anderson, Elaine S. 1977. Learning to speak with style. Ph.D. dissertation, Stanford University.

Basso, Keith. 1979. Portraits of "The Whiteman." Cambridge: Cambridge U. Press.

Bateson, Gregory. 1972. Steps to an ecology of mind. New York: Ballantine.

Bateson, Gregory. 1979. Mind and nature. New York: Ballantine.

Becker, Alton L. 1982. On Emerson on language. Analyzing discourse: Text and talk, Georgetown University Round Table on Languages and Linguistics 1981, ed. by Deborah Tannen, 1–11. Washington, DC: Georgetown U. Press.

Becker, A. L. 1979a. Text-building, epistemology, and aesthetics in Javanese Shadow Theatre. The imagination of reality, ed. by A. L. Becker & Aram Yengoyan, 211–243. Norwood, NJ: Ablex.

Becker, A. L. 1979b. The figure a sentence makes. Discourse and syntax, ed. by Talmy Givon, 243–259. New York: Academic Press.

Becker, A. L., and I Gusti Ngurah Oka. 1974. Person in Kawi: Exploration of an elementary semantic dimension. Oceanic Linguistics 13, 229–255.

Bennett, Adrian. 1978a. Interruptions and the interpretation of conversation. Proceedings of the fourth annual meeting of the Berkeley Linguistics Society, 557–575.

Bennett, Adrian. 1978b. Understanding conversation: The view through a phenomenological window. Ph.D. dissertation. University of California, Berkeley.

Bettelheim, Bruno. 1979. Surviving. New York: Knopf.

Bernstein, Basil. 1964. Elaborated and restricted codes: Their social origins and some consequences. American Anthropologist 66:6, part 2. 55–69.

Blom, Jan-Petter, and John J. Gumperz. 1972. Social meaning in linguistic structure: Code-switching in Norway. Directions in sociolinguistics, ed. by John Gumperz & Dell Hymes, 407–434. New York: Holt.

Bolinger, Dwight. 1976. Meaning and memory. Forum Linguisticum 1:1. 1–14.

177

Bright, William. 1982. Literature: Written and oral. Analyzing discourse: Text and talk, ed. by Deborah Tannen, 271–283. Georgetown University Round Table on Languages and Linguistics, 1981. Washington, DC: Georgetown U. Press.

Brown, Roger, and Albert Gilman. 1960. The pronouns of power and solidarity. Style in language, ed. by Thomas Sebeok, 253–276. Cambridge, MA: M.I.T. Press.

Brown, Penelope, and Stephen Levinson. 1978. Universals in language usage: Politeness phenomena. Questions and politeness, ed. by Esther Goody, 56–289. Cambridge: Cambridge U. Press.

Chafe, Wallace L. 1974. Language and consciousness. Language 50:1. 111–133.

Chafe, Wallace L. 1980. The deployment of consciousness in the production of a narrative. The pear stories: Cognitive, cultural, and linguistic aspects of narrative production, ed. by Wallace Chafe, 9–50. Norwood, NJ: Ablex.

Chafe, Wallace L. 1982. Integration and involvement in speaking, writing, and oral literature. Spoken and written language, ed. by Deborah Tannen, 35–53. Norwood, NJ: Ablex.

Condon, William S. 1963. Lexical-kinesic correlation. Ms. Pittsburgh: Western Psychiatric Institute.

Conley, John M., William M. O'Barr, and E. Allen Lind. 1979. The power of language: Presentational style in the courtroom. Duke Law Journal vol. 1978 no. 6.

Cook-Gumperz, Jenny. 1975. The child as practical reasoner. Sociocultural dimensions of language use, ed. by Mary Sanches & Ben Blount, 137–167. New York: Academic Press.

Cutler, Anne. 1974. On saying what you mean without meaning what you say. Papers from the Tenth Regional Meeting of the Chicago Linguistic Society.

Dreyfus, Jeff. 1975. Traffic's pretty heavy, huh? University of Michigan Department of Linguistics.

Durkheim, Emile. 1915. The elementary forms of the religious life. New York: The Free Press.

Erickson, Frederick. 1979. Talking down: Some cultural sources of miscommunication in interracial interviews. Nonverbal communication, ed. by Aaron Wolfgang, 99–126. New York: Academic Press.

Erickson, Frederick, and Jeffrey Shultz. 1982. The counselor as gatekeeper. New York: Academic.

Ervin-Tripp, Susan. 1972. On sociolinguistic rules: Alternation and co-occurrence. Directions in sociolinguistics, ed. by John Gumperz & Dell Hymes, 213–250. New York: Holt.

Ervin-Tripp, Susan, and Claudia Mitchell-Kernan (eds.). 1977. Child discourse. New York: Academic Press.

Esterly, Glenn. 1979. Slow talking in the big city. New West 4:11.67–72.

Falk, Jane. 1979. The conversational duet. Ph.D. dissertation, Princeton University.

Fillmore, Charles J. 1974. Pragmatics and the description of discourse. Pragmatik II, ed. by S. Schmidt, 83–104. Fink.

Fillmore, Charles J. 1976. The need for a frame semantics within linguistics. Statistical methods in linguistics, 5–29. Stockholm: Skriptor.

Fillmore, Lily Wong. 1976. The second time around. Ph.D. dissertation. Stanford University.

Fillmore, Lily Wong. 1979. Individual differences in language acquisition. Individual differences in language ability and language behavior, ed. by Charles J. Fillmore, Daniel Kempler, & William S.-Y. Wang, 203–228. New York: Academic Press.

Fowles, John. 1977. Daniel Martin. New York: Signet.

Frake, Charles O. 1977. Plying frames can be dangerous: Some reflections on methodology in cognitive anthropology. The Quarterly Newsletter of the Laboratory for Comparative Human Cognition, 1.1–7.

Friedrich, Paul. 1979. Poetic language and the imagination: Reformulation of the Sapir Hypothesis. Language, context, and the imagination, 441–512. Stanford, CA: Stanford U. Press.

Goffman, Erving. 1959. The presentation of self in everyday life. New York: Doubleday.

Goffman, Erving. 1967. Interaction ritual. Garden City, New York: Doubleday.

Goffman, Erving. 1974. Frame analysis. New York: Harper & Row.

Goffman, Erving. 1981. Response cries. Forms of talk, 78–123. Philadelphia: U. of Pennsylvania Press.

Goody, Jack, and Ian Watt. 1963. The consequences of literacy. Comparative studies in society and history 5.304–345.

Grice, H. P. 1967. Logic and conversation. William James Lectures, Harvard University. Rpt. Speech acts, ed. by Peter Cole & Jerry L. Morgan. New York: Academic, 1975.

Gumperz, John J. 1977. Sociocultural knowledge in conversational inference. Linguistics and anthropology, Georgetown University Round Table on Languages and Linguistics 1977, ed. by Muriel Saville-Troike, 191–211. Washington, DC: Georgetown U. Press.

Gumperz, John J. 1978a. Dialect and conversational inference in urban communication. Language in Society 7.393–409.

Gumperz, John J. 1978b. The conversational analysis of interethnic communication. Interethnic communication, ed. by E. Lamar Ross, 13–31. Southern Anthropological Society Proceedings, No. 12. Athens, GA: U. of Georgia Press.

Gumperz, John J. (ed.). 1982a. Language and social identity. Cambridge: Cambridge U. Press.

Gumperz, John J. 1982b. Discourse strategies. Cambridge: Cambridge U. Press.

Gumperz, John, and Deborah Tannen. 1979. Individual and social differences in language use. Individual differences in language ability and language behavior, ed. by Charles Fillmore, Daniel Kempler, & William S.-Y. Wang, 305–325. New York: Academic Press.

Halliday, M. A. K., and Ruqaiya Hasan. 1976. Cohesion in English. London: Longman.

Havelock, Eric. 1963. Preface to Plato. Cambridge, MA: Harvard U. Press.

Hymes, Dell. 1973. The scope of sociolinguistics. Report of the Twenty-Third Annual Round Table Meeting on Linguistics and Language Studies, ed. by Roger Shuy, 313–333. Washington, DC: Georgetown U. Press.

Hymes, Dell. 1974a. Ways of speaking. Explorations in the ethnography of speaking, ed. by Richard Bauman & Joel Sherzer, 433–451. Cambridge: Cambridge U. Press.

Hymes, Dell. 1974b. Foundations in sociolinguistics. Philadelphia: U. of Pennsylvania Press.

Keenan, Elinor, and Bambi B. Schieffelin. 1975. Topic as a discourse notion. Subject and topic, ed. by Charles N. Li, 335–384. New York: Academic Press.

Kochman, Thomas. 1981. Black and white styles in conflict. Chicago: U. of Chicago Press.

Labov, William. 1972. Language in the inner city. Philadelphia: U. of Pennsylvania Press.

Labov, William, and David Fanshel. 1977. Therapeutic discourse. New York: Academic Press.

Lakoff, George, and Mark Johnson. 1980. Metaphors we live by. Chicago: U. of Chicago Press.

Lakoff, Robin. 1973. The logic of politeness, or minding your p's and q's. Papers from the Ninth Regional Meeting of the Chicago Linguistics Society, 292–305.

Lakoff, Robin. 1975. Language and woman's place. New York: Harper & Row.

Lakoff, Robin Tolmach. 1976. Why you can't say what you mean. Review of Edwin Newman, Strictly speaking. Centrum 4:2.151–170.

Lakoff, Robin Tolmach. 1978. Review of Marshall Edelson, Language and interpretation in psychoanalysis. Language 54:2.377–394.

Lakoff, Robin Tolmach. 1979. Stylistic strategies within a grammar of style. Language, sex, and gender, ed. by Judith Orasanu, Mariam Slater, and Leonore Loeb Adler. Annals of the New York Academy of Science 327.53–78.

Lakoff, Robin Tolmach, and Deborah Tannen. In press. Conversational strategy and metastrategy in a pragmatic theory: The example of *Scenes from a Marriage*. Semiotica.

Michaels, Sarah, and Jenny Cook-Gumperz. 1979. A study of sharing time with first grade students: Discourse narratives in the classroom. Proceedings of the Fifth Annual Meeting of the Berkeley Linguistics Society, 51–80.

Mills, C. Wright. 1940. Situated action and vocabularies of motive. Symbolic interaction, ed. by Jerome G. Manis and Bernard N. Meltzer, 355–366. Boston: Allyn & Bacon, 1967.

Ochs, Elinor. 1979. Planned and unplanned discourse. Discourse and syntax, ed. by Talmy Givon, 51–80. New York: Academic Press.

Ochs, Elinor. 1982. Talking to children in Western Samoa. Language in Society 11:1.77–104.

Ochs, Elinor, and Bambi B. Schieffelin (eds.). 1979. Developmental pragmatics. New York: Academic Press.

Olson, David. 1977. From utterance to text: The bias of language in speech and writing. Harvard Educational Review 47:3.257–281.

Ong, Walter J., S. J. 1967. The presence of the word. New Haven, CT: Yale University Press.

Pask, Gordon. 1980. The limits of togetherness. Information processing 80, ed. by S. H. Lavington, 999–1012. The Hague: North-Holland Publishing Co.

Pittenger, Robert, Charles Hockett, and John Danehy. 1960. The first five minutes. Ithaca, New York: Paul Martineau.

Polanyi, Livia. 1978. False starts can be true. Proceedings of the Fourth Annual Meeting of the Berkeley Linguistics Society, 628–639.

Polanyi, Livia. 1979. So what's the point? Semiotica 25:3/4. 207–241.

Powers, John H. 1981. Conversational analysis and Susanne Langer's 'act' concept. Manuscript, Texas A & M.

Prince, Ellen. 1981. Toward a taxonomy of given-new information. Radical pragmatics, ed. by Peter Cole. New York: Academic Press.

Propp, Vladimir. 1958. Morphology of the folktale. Austin, TX: U. of Texas Press.

Rader, Margaret. 1982. Context in written language: The case of imaginative fiction. Spoken and written language, ed. by Deborah Tannen, 185–198. Norwood, NJ: Ablex.

Romaine, Suzanne, and Elizabeth Traugott. 1981. The problem of style in sociolinguistics. Paper presented at LSA winter meeting, New York.

Roy, Alice Myers. 1978. Irony in conversation. Ph.D. dissertation. U. of Michigan.

Ryave, Alan L. 1978. On the achievement of a series of stories. Studies in the organization of conversational interaction, ed. by Jim Schenkein, 113–132. New York: Academic Press.

Sacks, Harvey. 1971. Unpublished lecture notes, March 11, 1971.

Sacks, Harvey, and Emanuel Schegloff. 1974. Opening up closings. Ethnomethodology, ed. by Roy Turner. Baltimore, MD: Penguin.

Sacks, Harvey, Emanuel A. Schegloff, and Gail Jefferson. 1974. A simplest systematics for the organization of turntaking for conversation. Language 50:4.696–735.

Sapir, Edward. 1958. Speech as a personality trait. Selected writings of Edward Sapir in language, culture, and personality, ed. by David Mandelbaum. Berkeley: U. of California Press.

Saville-Troike, Muriel. 1980. Cross-cultural communication in the classroom. Georgetown University Round Table on Languages and Linguistics 1980, ed. by James E. Alatis, 348–355. Washington, DC: Georgetown U. Press.

Schenkein, Jim. 1978. Studies in the organization of conversational interaction. New York: Academic Press.

Schieffelin, Bambi B. 1979. How Kaluli children learn what to say, what to do, and how to feel: An ethnographic study of the development of communicative competence. Ph.D. dissertation. Columbia U.

Scollon, Ron. In press. The machine stops: Silence in the metaphor of malfunction. Perspectives on silence, ed. by Deborah Tannen & Muriel Saville-Troike. Norwood, NJ: Ablex.

Scollon, Ron. 1982. The rhythmic integration of ordinary talk. Analyzing discourse: Text and talk. Georgetown University Round Table on Languages and Linguistics 1981, ed. by Deborah Tannen, 335–349. Washington, DC: Georgetown U. Press.

Scollon, Ron, and Suzanne B. K. Scollon. 1981. Athabaskan English interethnic communication. Narrative, literacy and face in interethnic communication, 11–37. Norwood, NJ: Ablex.

Shultz, Jeffrey, Susan Florio, and Frederick Erickson. 1982. Where's the floor? Aspects of the cultural organization of social relationships in communication at home and at school. Ethnography and education: Children in and out of school, ed. by Perry Gilmore & Alan Glatthorn, 88–123. Washington, DC: Center for Applied Linguistics.

Tannen, Deborah. 1975. Communication mix and mixup, or how linguistics can ruin a marriage. San Jose State Occasional Papers in Linguistics, 205–211. San Jose, CA: San Jose State U.

Tannen, Deborah. 1979. What's in a frame? Surface evidence for underlying expectations. New dimensions in discourse processes, ed. by Roy Freedle, 137–181. Norwood, NJ: Ablex.

Tannen, Deborah. 1980. A comparative analysis of oral narrative strategies. The pear stories, Cognitive, cultural, and linguistic aspects of narrative production, ed. by Wallace Chafe, 51–87. Norwood, NJ: Ablex.

Tannen, Deborah. 1981a. Indirectness in discourse: Ethnicity as conversational style. Discourse Processes 4:3. 221–238.

Tannen, Deborah. 1981b. New York Jewish conversational style. International Journal of the Sociology of Language 30.133–139.

Tannen, Deborah. 1981c. The machine-gun question: An example of conversational style. Journal of Pragmatics. 5:5.383–397.

Tannen, Deborah. 1982. Oral and literate strategies in spoken and written narratives. Language 58:1.1–21.

Tannen, Deborah. 1983. When is an overlap not an interruption. The First Delaware

Symposium on Language Studies, ed. by Robert Di Pietro, William Frawley, & Alfred Wedel, 19–129. Newark, DE: U. of Delaware Press.

Tannen, Deborah. In press-a. Relative focus on involvement in spoken and written discourse. Literacy, language and learning: The nature and consequences of reading and writing, ed. by David Olson. Cambridge: Cambridge U. Press.

Tannen, Deborah. In press-b. Frames and schemas in discourse analysis of interaction. *Quaderni di Semantica.*

Tannen, Deborah, and Muriel Saville-Troike (eds.). In press. Functions of silence. Norwood, NJ: Ablex.

Tannen, Deborah, and Cynthia Wallat. 1983. Doctor/mother/child communication: Linguistic analysis of a pediatric interaction. The social organization of doctor/patient communication, ed. by Sue Fisher and Alexandra Dundas Todd, 203–219. Washington, DC: Center for Applied Linguistics.

Tyler, Stephen. 1978. The said and the unsaid. New York: Academic Press.

Van Valin, Robert. 1977. Meaning and interpretation. Manuscript. Temple University.

Vassiliou, Vasso, Harry Triandis, George Vassiliou, and Howard McGuire. 1972. Interpersonal contact and stereotyping. The analysis of subjective culture, ed. by Harry Triandis, 89–115. New York: Wiley.

Wallat, Cynthia, and Deborah Tannen. 1982. The dilemma of parent participation in medical settings: A linguistic analysis. Presented at American Sociological Association Annual Meeting, San Francisco, September 1982.

Watzlawick, Paul, Janet Helmick Beavin, and Don D. Jackson. 1967. The pragmatics of human communication. New York: Norton.

Winograd, Terry. 1976. An analysis of the 'fainting on the subway' text. Manuscript, Stanford University.

Yngve, Victor H. 1970. On getting a word in edgewise. Sixth Regional Meeting of the Chicago Linguistics Society. 567–577.

Young, Linda Wai Ling. 1982. Inscrutability revisited. Language and social identity, ed. by John J. Gumperz, 72–84. Cambridge: Cambridge U. Press.

Author Index

Subject Index